MAYBE TEACHING IS A BAD IDEA

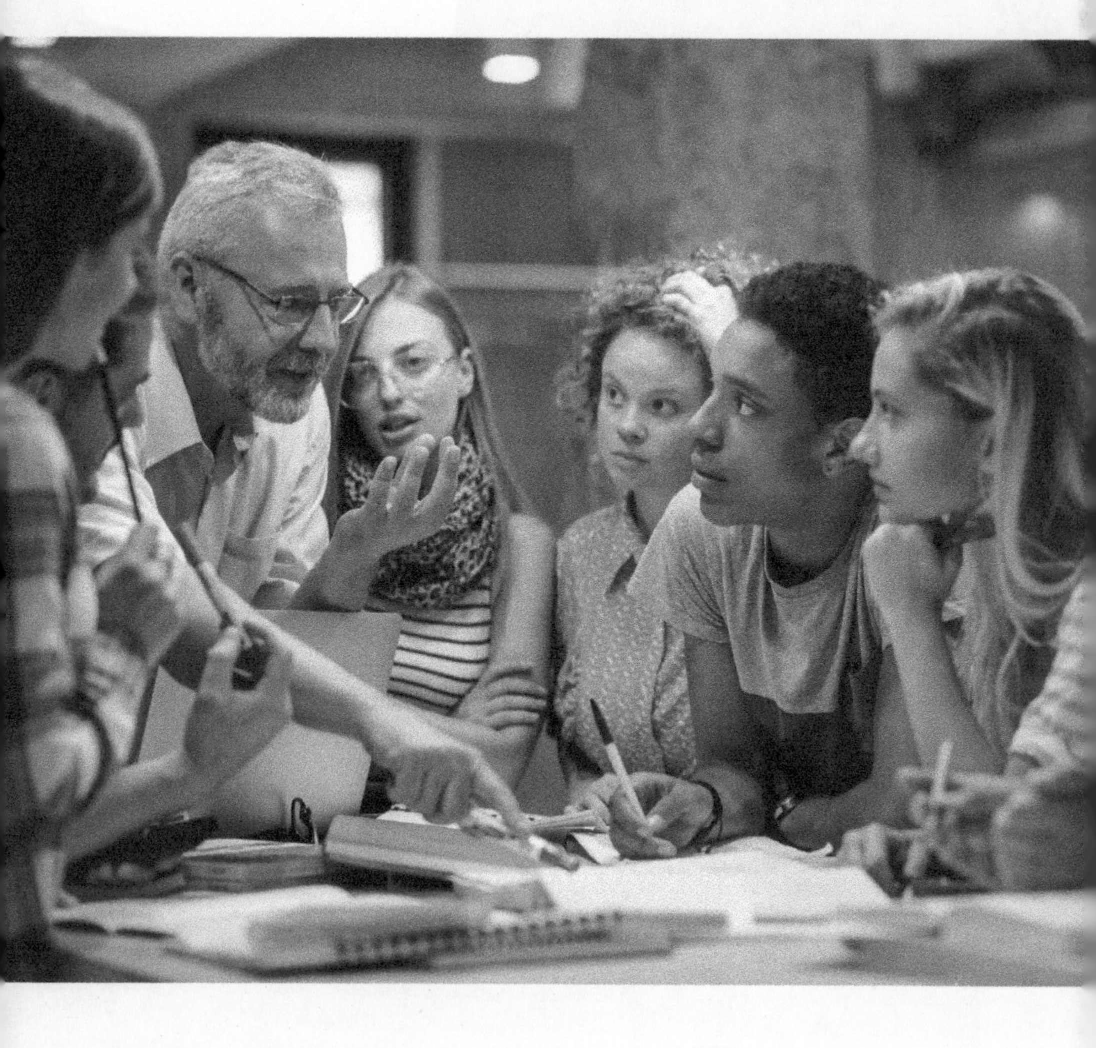

MAYBE TEACHING IS A BAD IDEA

Why Faculty Should Focus on Learning

Larry D. Spence

Introduction by Maryellen Weimer

STERLING, VIRGINIA

COPYRIGHT © 2022 BY STYLUS PUBLISHING, LLC.

Published by Stylus Publishing, LLC
22883 Quicksilver Drive
Sterling, Virginia 20166-2019

All rights reserved. No part of this book may be reprinted or reproduced in any form or by any electronic, mechanical, or other means, now known or hereafter invented, including photocopying, recording, and information storage and retrieval, without permission in writing from the publisher.

Library of Congress Cataloging-in-Publication Data

Names: Spence, Larry D. (Larry David), 1936-2018 author.
Title: Maybe teaching is a bad idea : why faculty should focus on learning / Larry D. Spence ; introduction my Maryellen Weimer
Description: First edition. | Sterling, Virginia : Stylus, 2022. | Includes bibliographical references and index. | Summary: "Deep and lasting learning results when we teach human brains in ways responsive to how they're structured and how they function, which is not how we imagine they work or wish they would work. This book proposes a radical restructuring of teaching so that it conforms to how people learn"-- Provided by publisher.
Identifiers: LCCN 2022019692 (print) | LCCN 2022019693 (ebook) | ISBN 9781642674644 (cloth) | ISBN 9781642674651 (paperback) | ISBN 9781642674668 (pdf) | ISBN 9781642674675 (epub)
Subjects: LCSH: Cognitive learning. | Effective teaching. | College teaching. | Knowledge, Theory of.
Classification: LCC LB1062 .S74 2022 (print) | LCC LB1062 (ebook) | DDC 370.15--dc23/eng/20220609
LC record available at https://lccn.loc.gov/2022019692
LC ebook record available at https://lccn.loc.gov/2022019693

13-digit ISBN: 978-1-64267-464-4 (cloth)
13-digit ISBN: 978-1-64267-465-1 (paperback)
13-digit ISBN: 978-1-64267-466-8 (library networkable e-edition)
13-digit ISBN: 978-1-64267-467-5 (consumer e-edition)

Printed in the United States of America

All first editions printed on acid free paper that meets the American National Standards Institute Z39-48 Standard.

Bulk Purchases

Quantity discounts are available for use in workshops and for staff development.

Call 1-800-232-0223

First Edition, 2022

CONTENTS

ACKNOWLEDGMENTS

This book is the culmination of a dream of Larry's before he died following a brief illness in 2018. Without the persistent efforts of Maryellen Weimer and Bruce Parker who laboriously combed through his mostly finished manuscript, editing and proofreading as they pieced it together for publication, it would never have seen the light of day. During the years he was working on it, Larry had been discussing his ideas with the two of them. He and Maryellen met regularly to talk about his experiences in the classroom that evolved into a theory of how to teach students to develop their own positions and arguments. The techniques he used are explained in this book.

When Maryellen decided she would try to get his book published with the help of David Brightman who had edited some of her books, I knew she was taking on a huge task. She acknowledged that, but she'd made a commitment to Larry to do so before he died. I later suggested she contact Bruce as a second reader, which she did, and they worked together on the final draft.

My heartfelt thanks to all of you for your hard work and dedication.

—Maya Spence

INTRODUCTION

Maryellen Weimer

Author Larry Spence, an associate professor of political science at Penn State, was recognized for distinguished teaching with two university-wide teaching awards and one from the College of Liberal Arts. After 25 years teaching, he became the founding director of the university's Schreyer Institute for Innovation in Learning. Upon his retirement, he directed a series of learning initiatives in Penn State's School of Information Sciences and Technology and The Smeal College of Business. He died as he was working on the final chapter of this book.

If you're interested in a new vision of education—a unique way of describing what happens when instructors teach and students learn—you'll find it in this book. Unfortunately, a great deal of what's written about postsecondary education is a rehash of what appears elsewhere. Currently popular ideas, trendy notions, catch phrases, and buzz words recycle endlessly, but they don't appear in this book.

It's an academic book in the sense of doing what's expected in scholarly work. It develops and advances arguments, cites supportive references, and offers illustrative examples. Larry builds a strong case against current instructional practices—he makes points persuasively and with passion.

But in other ways, it's not at all like most academic books. What concerns Larry about teaching and learning grew out of his experiences as a student and as a teacher, and the book recounts those experiences—his first memories of school, how he learned to read, his lackluster performance in high school, failure in college, and his first teaching experiences. What happened in his courses and various interactions and encounters with students, colleagues, and administrators raised more questions. Larry doesn't tell war stories—mostly he recounts failures, challenges, and mistakes, and his struggles to learn from them. His narratives make the book distinctive; they add interest, bits of humor, and make it a hard book to put down. "I spent my career working out the ideas I'm writing about in this book," Larry once told me. What he experienced became the cauldron in which the book's ideas boiled.

It's a provocative piece of scholarship. In a tone neither gentle nor accommodating, Larry rails against long-held assumptions and educational practices. Disgruntled with the way things are in light of the ways they could be, Larry can sound like a curmudgeon. Almost nothing about the way colleges and universities operate pleases him. But the book isn't a hopeless rant. Larry envisions a different kind of educational experience for students and teachers. In chapter 6 he candidly admits, "My vision of teaching was not only unpopular, but I also wasn't convinced it was right and it was surely misunderstood." The book offers an evolving vision of teaching and learning in higher education.

Don't expect to agree with everything in the book. Rather, anticipate challenges, pokes, and prods that aren't always gentle. Expect to feel responsible for figuring out how your beliefs and those of others have shaped your instructional practice. Larry writes near the end of chapter 4, "I wanted to write a book that asked real questions and explored possible answers. I am not concerned that you agree with my answers or ideas, but I fervently hope the questions I'm raising will lead you to questions about habitual teaching practices and the resulting failure of students to learn" (p. 55). The book's ideas regularly consumed me. After one especially stimulating exchange with Larry, I found myself driving home to a house I hadn't lived in for 10 years.

It's a book with ideas that beg to be discussed with others. Will what Larry's proposing work at the kind of institution where you teach? Is it an approach any teacher can undertake, or does it demand a certain level of instructional maturity? How representative are Larry's experiences in school? Does the idea of the teacher coach work with all kinds of content? How representative is Larry as a learner? Is he at all like any of your students? Do you agree with the implications for teaching Larry draws from how brains function?

What happened in Larry's classrooms raised questions he then sought to answer by reading, study, and application. He epitomizes our notions of a reflective practitioner. The classroom was his laboratory. There he worked out the details of a coaching model of teaching. It's the account of how clear-eyed observations of learning and teaching, and reflection on past educational experiences set one teacher on a Don Quixote quest to find a better way to teach—one that's true to how people learn.

And finally, just a bit about what isn't in the book. It's not a how to teach manual. Larry mentions some instructional strategies, but rather than a nuts and bolts diagram, this book takes a big picture look at a radically different approach to education. Like many futuristic visions, it describes a place far from where we are and doesn't hand us a GPS. That's another reason for talking about the book. Larry leaves us to map the way to the very learning-centered place he envisions.

An Overview

Here's four of Larry's paragraphs that aptly summarize his work. "This book presents a critique of the failed teaching models that dominate our schools and universities and offers an alternative model of learning that focuses on prior knowledge and failures. Books on teaching tell us that a critical task for instructors is to assess what students know and believe in order to build on their knowledge. Teachers need to figure out if what students know is accurate and relevant, and if it's not, they need to fill in knowledge gaps and correct misunderstandings.

In fact, that describes the student's task. It's not one teachers can do. Students must assess what they know, don't know, and need to know. To be blunt, teaching cannot and should not be aimed at transferring knowledge from teacher brains into student brains. Decades of experience have made perfectly clear that this approach frustrates teachers, bores students, and results in minimal learning.

Deep and lasting learning results when we teach human brains responsive to how they're structured and how they function, which is not how we imagine they work or wish they would work. This book proposes a radical restructuring of teaching so that it conforms to how people learn. All flesh-and-blood humans have theories, models, principles, and rules that guide their actions, what I call stories, maps, and models. More formally, they're referred to as *representations*. They are how we make sense of the world around us and inside us. Some representations are explicit theories based on science or practical experience. But many are informal, not articulated, and operate below consciousness. In the aggregate, such representations constitute human knowledge. As such, they govern most of our day-to-day choices. *Learning is the process of repairing or enhancing our representations—building better models that explain things more accurately, deeply, and broadly.*

But learning is not automatic. We have to decide to challenge our representations. Often, we do this as a result of failure. As children, we fell, babbled, and broke things. Spontaneously we revised our expectations and the assumptions that drove them. As we get older, the revision and repair of our models gets more difficult. We would rather avoid failure than confront it. We forget how much can be learned from mistakes. Indeed, this is the way we learn—we doubt some part of our knowledge, try to understand what might be wrong, and then design strategic failures to find what we must change to be more successful. Learning through use is necessary if we want students to be creative and self-teaching. This book lays out a coaching methodology that, if implemented, will enhance students' abilities to become lifetime self-teachers, the true goal of education."

These central ideas unfold across the book's chapters. They move forward and back through the years of his career. Less linear and more winding, the ideas spiral around each other, tightly connected but with the relationships revealed as the ideas are pulled through the various chapters. It's not a book that makes much sense if you just read one chapter or if you read them out of order. Some ideas regularly mentioned don't get unpacked and fit into the vision until later in the book. It's a book best understood once it's considered in its entirety. In preparation for what's to come, here's a brief preview of each chapter.

Chapter 1—Early Learning Experiences in School

Larry starts school and it's not what he expected. He experiences transfer teaching. It's teaching that tells and lauds correct answers. He argues against it for the rest of the book. In its place, he proposes instruction that better fits how the brain learns.

Chapter 2—Early Teaching Experiences in College

Larry discovers he wants to teach and shares his first experiences doing so. Much to his dismay, he finds himself teaching as he was taught. He does most of the talking, assigns essays, directs discussion, gives tests, and grades papers. He switches to an "action to knowledge" instructional approach and discovers that his students know more than he or they reckoned.

Chapter 3—It's Time to Put Lectures on the Shelf

Like most students, Larry listened to lots of lectures. They bored him and he regularly slept through them. Despite extensive evidence against lecturing, Larry lectures, even admits he enjoys doing so. An experience in one of his classes makes it clear that there's only one way teachers can improve lectures: Talk less.

Chapter 4—What's the Role of Questions in Learning?

Teachers ask the questions, not students—evidence verifies that claim. They do so assuming that asking encourages students to question. That's what Larry believed. Then he considered how babies learn—by asking a steady stream of questions. From the answers their brains chose, they match and build "representations," maps or models that become their understandings of reality.

Chapter 5—Content: Does All That Information Lead to Knowledge?

More content in a course does not automatically result in more learning. Confused thinking about information and knowledge leads many to believe that mountains of information (big data) somehow stack up and become higher knowledge. Larry calls for a knowledge revolution.

Chapter 6—Teaching Realities: Conflicts, Assumptions, and Approaches

Strong among teaching realities is the resistance to change and innovation. Two approaches remain the dominant teaching traditions: performance teaching and transmission teaching. Flaws in both hinder learning. Larry proposes a coaching mode based on the premise that knowledge is something learners must build for themselves.

Chapter 7—What Is Learning?

It's a word used all the time and without any sense of confusion, but the simpler the conceptions of learning, the more enigmatic it becomes. Here Larry argues for more complex ways of understanding learning, and he finds those in the cognitive revolution. He narrates his experiences learning to read, and uses them to illustrate how brains are unique and do not need teachers to learn.

Chapter 8—Rethinking Failure and Ignorance

Learners need to stop avoiding failure and recognize that ignorance surrounds them. It's time to stop being embarrassed by what isn't known. Convinced that failure and ignorance can be instrumental in learning, Larry tries to correct student mistakes and experiences the consequences. He takes a turn at learning from failure.

Chapter 9—Criticism: The Key to Learning

A teacher taught Larry the value of criticism. But it's not an easy skill to learn and it's a difficult one to teach. Many of the attempts to teach critical thinking have failed or barely succeeded. Larry attempts to do so using Meehan's theory of knowledge which offers criteria for critical thinking. It allows Larry to further develop his coaching model.

Chapter 10—Teaching That Promotes Learning From Mistakes and Failure

Three instructional approaches support efforts to learn from failure; active learning, in Dewey's sense of learning by doing; Minimalism, a design-based approach to learning that prescribes less instruction and more support; and greater reliance on the imagination for potential solutions, alternative explanations, and other possible answers.

Chapter 11—Practice Makes Perfect, but Not Unless It's Deliberate

Larry relates how he "learned" chemistry through deliberate practice. It did not happen in school. Ericsson, credited with current thinking on deliberate practice, maintains that the focus should be on the most difficult and mistake-prone aspects of a performance. Larry lays out how teacher-coaches can design tasks, specify goals, and provide error-focused feedback thereby encouraging deliberate practice.

Some Further Explanation

Larry was in his late 70s and early 80s when he wrote the book. His health started to decline, but "we're not wasting our time together talking about it," he would say when I asked how he was doing. A couple of months before he died, he closed our conversation by quietly observing, "You may have to finish the book." I promised I would and felt like I could. I'd been after him to do the book for some time. We worked together on the proposal which was originally contracted by another publisher. Various deadlines passed as he labored on intently exploring and refining his ideas, and forever reading something else he thought might be relevant. We met monthly to discuss whatever chapter he was working on. Before a session at Cool Beans (our local coffee shop) Larry would send draft material, I'd read it, and we'd discuss it, well, mostly argue about it. Larry shared parts of the manuscript with various colleagues and friends—he was hungry for feedback, although he routinely started by disagreeing with any objections made by those of us who read the chapters.

I didn't anticipate that finishing the book would be quite as challenging as it's turned out to be. Larry was working on a second draft. The first draft came in at something around 750 pages for a book contracted not to exceed 300 pages. "Don't send me a chapter that you haven't cut in half," I chided. The manuscript as he left it was about 400 pages, and this book is considerably shorter. Larry loved to follow ideas around, starting with their point of origin, outlining how they evolved, where they'd digressed, what else they'd led to, and their current status. Near the end of the chapter where Larry recounts how he learned to read, he notes, "Since I write much the way I learned to read, we must hope that I can pare away enough meanderings and amusing dead-ends to present an attractive narrative." Hopefully I've helped Larry accomplish that goal.

It was such an honor to edit what the author considered his most important work and so wrenching that he could no longer speak for it. Without Larry I sliced and diced sections, fussed with the order of the chapters, and rewrote section titles. Larry liked to just launch chapters—often with a story. I tried to make the point that readers like to know where they're headed when a chapter begins. I don't think Larry agreed but some of these chapters now have introductions that I've written. Others have transitions between sections that I've inserted, and most of the mentions to material that appears elsewhere in the book, are ones I added. I found myself regularly talking to Larry about the need for these changes—in the silence that followed, I missed him.

When I first started working on the book, I struggled to make changes. It felt like I was violating something that belonged to another. I fixed proofreading errors and anguished over what I thought really needed to be done. When I talked to Larry's spouse Maya about my reluctance, she recommended I get in touch with Larry's lifelong friend, Bruce Parker. They'd met as graduate students at Berkeley. Bruce turned out to be a godsend—a retired lawyer who took Larry and the manuscript to task. "This doesn't make any sense." "I have no idea what Larry is talking about here." "Is he ever going to get to the point?" Bruce empowered me to make the changes we both felt were necessary to showcase Larry's interesting and revolutionary ideas about teaching and learning.

We did debate whether we should add material that clarified Larry's views on certain topics. For example, Larry believed the point of education was to get students so that they could do something. He wanted teachers to create conditions in which students could practice applying "knowledge and information to successfully solve problems in real-world conditions." But Larry did not believe the only legitimate university programs were those that prepared students for specific careers. His ideas about learning by doing were similar to those of Dewey—students should learn to think critically by doing it—not by listening to others do it or reading examples. We ended up adding very little to the text; sometimes a definition, explanatory phrase, or sentence, but this is Larry's book—we've left his ideas as he left them.

One of my biggest challenges involved tracking down the references. Larry hadn't yet completed a reference list, often just inserting a name and date in the text. In some cases, I could not locate quotations or match the dates Larry had in the text with publications. In those cases, when possible, I referenced work that illustrates or supports what Larry has in the text.

Larry did not do a dedication for the book. Those of us who know him suspect he would have dedicated the book to his students. Many of them kept in touch and he took great joy in their accomplishments. Stories about them and comments from them appear throughout the book. He regularly credited students with the most important lessons he learned about teaching. But probably the person most deserving of the book's dedication is Maya. Larry could talk about the book's contents at great length, and Maya listened, asked questions, and offered advice. She was there for every chapter. I don't think the book would have happened without her.

I would like to say thanks again to Larry's friend, Bruce Parker, for his help with the manuscript, to Mark Robertson for work on the references, to Lisa Lenz for tracking down career information, and to Maya, for her encouragement and patience—I promised to be done with the manuscript long before I was.

I

EARLY LEARNING EXPERIENCES IN SCHOOL

Born in the great depression, he was a cheerful first grandchild. He came from two large farming families. His father, who didn't farm, donated half his paycheck to support his eight brothers and sisters. His mother struggled through childhood among 13 siblings on a hardscrabble West Virginia farm. Aunts, uncles, and grandparents blessed him with stories, riddles, songs, and the hard rules of work. His luxuries were people and words.

He couldn't wait to go to school. There you learned. When his mother read to him each night before bed worlds opened. Swiss girls ate cheese and milk, giants ate Englishmen, and Trolls ate goats. Tailors, dwarfs, match girls, shepherds, Indians, pioneers, elves, and dragons talked, sang, fumed, and fought. This was the world of castles and claymores that he wanted to enter. Hungrily he watched the preacher wave his big black Bible on Sunday; hungrily he ran his hands over the spines of his father's encyclopedias and traced the letters in the cartoon balloons in the daily paper. The desires, quick adventures, and bravery of those printed words called him like siren melodies.

Finally, that first day of school arrived. Starched and spotless, he marched off alone to enter the world of school. It was 1942. He walked down the street, waved at the neighbors watching from their porches, turned left at the streetcar line, and crossed the highway to stop at a seedy grocery. There he handed over 10 cents for a thick pencil and a tablet with a red lion on the cover. One more block took him to the Emerson Elementary School—a foreboding redbrick building in the middle of a grassless playground. He rushed up the steep worn steps.

Inside was cool and dark. Down an oiled wood corridor, following his mother's directions, (he was determined to go to school on his own) he found his homeroom. Battered tablet desks and worktables faced the teacher's oak fortress. He found one lone desk beside it. To be near the teacher, he sat there, opened the tablet, held the pencil and watched his classmates arrive. They filled the seats and stared at him. Silence fell when a large woman walked in, looked at the class and then stepped in front of the boy. "What's your name?"

"Larry."

"Larry what?"

"Larry David Spence," he answered.

"You mean Lawrence."

"No, it's Larry because . . ."

"And why are you seated in the dunce seat?"

"To be near a teacher." Titters and giggles enveloped the class.

"Quiet! Quiet!" She glared at the class and turned again to face him. "You sit here when you can't stay in your seat, when you talk to your neighbor, or when you don't pay attention. I don't want to see you here again, understand?"

He nodded as laughs from around the room slipped through lips and fingers. She shoved him firmly toward a table of boys in the farthest corner. He dragged his new shoes to a seat.

"Hi, Larry" said a boy in overalls.

Relieved to escape the teacher's attention, he asked questions about the dunce chair, the teacher's name, where the books were, what you did all day, and when lunch was. His gangly companions, some repeating the grade, laughed and told him he was surely dumb.

He felt the shadow before he saw it.

"No one," sliced her voice, "talks in this room without permission. Understand?"

He slumped as she marched back to her desk. This couldn't be the place. Learning was talk. Learning was questions. Learning was getting answers and stories and doing new things. He followed uncles, aunts, grandparents, and parents—even neighbors and garbage men—and asked them about what they were doing and they explained their marvels. He talked to passing strangers on the street; asked them where they lived, what they did, and who they were. Most were delighted to answer and became new friends. He loved questions. They were like looking out windows, peeking into cracks, or walking through doors.

School, it turned out, was a place where teachers talked. They asked questions, gave orders, hurried you, described your faults, while bestowing "good jobs," "take your seats," "not now's," and "well done's." To stay seated was exalted. Everyone did the same thing at the same time—looked at the same picture, drew the same tree, said the same words, and sang the same song. But if you looked out the window, talked to a neighbor, picked up another book, drew a bloody pirate, or gazed over the bent heads, the dunce seat got you.

Before school happened to him, times of nothing going on let him relax, watch, or make. He would trace a beetle's path, walk to a neighbor's place for a chat, examine a worm to see which end was a head, cut out magazine pictures, or hammer wooden cheese boxes into trucks. To be alone then was a delight, but in school, surrounded by classmates, he was lonely. Confined to chairs, he sent his thoughts to the blue sky. With practice, he could look studious and be gone. He fastened his eyes to pages he did not see, on numbers he would not read and on teachers he refused to hear. Instead, he would visit his grandfather's green farm fields of corn, tobacco rows, and the brown eyes of milk cows chewing cud. Unspoken fantasies made life durable. But the better the worlds imagined the more wrenching his return to school.

First grade marched into the brown, orange, and red of fall. The colors fell from the trees, swept along the street, and piled against the curbs. He kicked the golden leaves into motley showers as he walked mechanically to Mrs. Summit's classroom.

"Today we will color scenes from autumn." The line drawings of pumpkins, cornstalks, boys, girls, ubiquitous dogs, and Farmer Jones were passed out.

"And what are the colors of autumn?" intoned Mrs. Summit as she distributed the assortment of stubby crayons.

Mercedes said, "Brown."

"Right. You, Dane, other colors?"

"Green."

"No, not much. What did you see on your way to school today, Larry?"

"Nothing."

"Anyone, what are the other colors of autumn that Larry didn't see?"

"Orange, red, yellow," the chorus went on as she walked to her desk.

"Now work quietly. Let's see if you can color these sheets to look like October."

He grabbed a black crayon. Shoes: four black smudges on the ends of the children's legs; coal lump eyes and a hurried mouth on the pumpkin; two black dots on a dog; and two stumps of boots on Farmer Jones. The empty white space of the road invited and a kidney shaped blackness emerged. It made him smile.

He looked at the faces on the sheet. You were supposed to leave them white. Nobody's face was white—they were pink, orange, tan, or blotched with red and stippled with black. When he colored at home he used a red crayon lightly to render them pink—sort of. He tried a blunt red crayon on the girl's face. Hand slipped and a red scar slashed her nose. Rubbing smeared it. His belly tightened. This would be another bad score, maybe a "poor," and maybe a move back to the bad student table in the corner. Not wanting the mistake to show, he pressed down on the crayon to cover the girl's face. It became blood red and not neat. Now the picture was wrong, he couldn't make it right, so it didn't matter what he did. In the freedom of despair he added yellow hair to the bright red face. The boy had to match, then the farmer. Laboring away he began to see autumn. The picture swirled red, yellow, green leaves and golden rod punctuated by black holes. The colors surged beyond the lines into a tapestry. It was full of mistakes. It shouted failure. It pleased him.

A deep quiet made him sense she was near. Mrs. Summit's hand whisked the paper high above the table. Classmates tittered. "And what is this, Larry? These don't look like people; the faces are all red?"

"They aren't people. They are drawings."

"And why all red?"

"I dunno."

"And why? Why don't you know?"

Her questions fired at him in a tommy-gun staccato. He knew the routine. Teachers asked: But never could he get a question in. Never could he ask: Why are we doing this? When do we start reading? Why can't we make up our own stories?

"Why are these faces red?"

"Why not?" he exploded. "Why can't I make them red? What if I made them blue?"

With his arm she yanked him to the dunce seat. Larry had disturbed the class, she announced. That day, he took a note to his parents requesting a meeting. When they came 2 days later, Mrs. Summit showed them the page and suggested that their son might be troubled. Maybe they should seek counseling.

"Well, why did you color those faces red?" his mother asked when she they came home.

"It was a mistake, Momma."

"What happened?"

"I wanted to make them pink with a red crayon. I pressed too hard."

"What about that black hole?"

And he smiled, "It was a puddle."

At home and in his neighborhood Larry learned with excitement and joy. In school he was taught; expected to stay seated, stay quiet, and answer questions. "The drive to learn in humans is something so strong, so defining of human nature. . . that it should still amaze us as truly remarkable that we have been able to design a social institution that can teach children to fail at learning," writes Ruth Paradise (1998, pp. 276–277). Larry was up against that institution. He was supposed to conform and please an embattled teacher. The innovative reformer, Seymour Papert (1980), notes: "Children, until they get to school, are avid, eager, successful learners. Then, when they come to school, the learning is not so good."

In this book I want to explore that conflict, not to revile teachers or educators or even to celebrate students but to understand why it exists and how we have come to accept it. Daniel Willingham (2017), the cognitive scientist, asks *Why Don't Students Like School?* as the title of his book on how the mind works. The question presupposes the conflict. His short answer is that students' minds (and all our minds) are defective learning devices. I propose a different question: "Why don't schools like students?"

Transmission Teaching Didn't Work for Me and Doesn't Work for Others

Transmission or transfer teaching exploits what instructors know but ignores what students know. Student knowledge is incomplete, often inaccurate. Mrs. Summit would say, "That's why they're students!" Their need for more and better knowledge tempts teachers to skip the student's hard work of reorganizing their knowledge by presenting them with a whole new package of better organized information. When teachers take that approach, it makes what students know an obstacle. When Mrs. Summit interrogated students, she knew the "right" answer and that's what she expected students to deliver. My failure to do so, got me in all sorts of trouble.

In transfer teaching questions investigate student knowledge: Did students get the message? Did they read? Can they interpret? Are they diligent? Questions like these assume that the human brain is defective. Although few now claim that student brains are blank, to most instructors they are defaced. Transmitting knowledge begins with erasures. To fill students with ideas that they don't know they need, we must dismiss what they know. Interrogating clears the way for students to learn. But this sets off a war, one that lasted for years in my case. No one can give up what they know without risking madness. Instead, students avoid and minimalize new knowledge. And that makes teachers think they aren't capable learners.

Teachers need to begin with what students already know. That knowledge may be immature, but it is the beginning of all efforts. Tell a preschooler that the earth is round, and he will learn that we all live on a pancake. Correct him, explaining that you mean we live on a spinning sphere and he will learn that the pancake sits on a ball. Such errors are not always predictable. Each student lives off schemas and images based on their unique minds and experiences. The initial and sometimes lasting results of learning can be bizarre. For example, if we teach that plants need "food" then students may think they must feed them dirt. If we assert that the varied positions of the earth cause seasonal temperature changes then students likely will infer that the earth moves from near to quite far away from the sun. In short, students distort or ignore novel information and patterns to conserve the integrity of their knowledge. They change their knowledge only when it enables them to think and act more effectively—and they are the judges of that.

In the college classroom teachers mostly teach as they were taught. That's what I did when I started teaching, as I explain in chapter 2. The transmission model of teaching and learning is therefore over-learned. It truncates the range of available choice. Even worse, when new techniques are introduced, they are undermined by old habits. Thus, when reformers promote classroom discussion instead of lectures, a less effective hybrid results—discussions conducted with teachers asking all the questions.

We need to step outside traditional models and think of instructors as designers creating contexts that promote student questions. What students need is a range of freedom that allows them to try out their ideas and learn from mistakes. That requires a different configuration of resources, routines, and demands. Time consuming and demanding as it may be, the design of learning contexts requires alternative theories of knowledge, practice, reasoning, and information as we shall delve into in the chapters ahead. It is also a wonderful challenge to our imagination—one that calls for teachers and professors to be more curious about classroom failures. Classrooms could become laboratories. Here's a wonderful illustration of how that can work.

We Learn by Building Our Own Views of the World

Seymour Sarason was a Yale professor of psychology who for over 6 decades produced some 40 sympathetic, but adamant, books critical of American school reforms. Hours observing classroom culture showed him that many teaching routines hindered learning. Reviewing years of attempts to change those routines he concluded that in reforming education, "the more things change, the more things stay the same."

His skepticism about traditional education emerged early in his academic career. A new PhD, Sarason was a clinical psychologist at a school for the mentally compromised. He was assigned to assist a visiting German scholar, Henry Schaefer-Simmern, conduct art classes. Schaefer was a visual artist and a scholar of Gestalt psychology, which posited that innate mental laws determined the way we see things. He believed artistic ability was basic to human nature. Every mind had the capacity to transform perceptual experiences into artistic forms. Schaefer wanted to demonstrate that humans—even those considered defective—could make genuine art.

For Schaeffer, traditional art education strangled creativity. By assuming that art begins with copying reality, it ignored both the inner process of visual conceiving and the immense complexity of the world. He thought people could develop an internal aesthetic by working through developmental stages (Schaefer-Simmern, 1948). To create a striking image the artist ignores many unnecessary details, concentrates on a few meaningful features, and conveys them clearly to inform us about the observed "thing."

Schaefer wanted to test his theory of universal artistic ability by conducting classes for mentally compromised patients. He taught two studio art classes two or three times per week. As Sarason describes the class, around eight students worked on individual drawings for several hours. Each student's project—a drawing, painting, or design—was unique. They would work away, stop to study their work, maybe get another sheet of paper to start over, or turn to talk with another student. Schaefer wrote at his desk or talked with individual students about their creations when they brought them to him for comments.

He discussed their projects and asked questions he didn't know the answers to: "What do you want to do now?" "What do you like about your picture?" "How could you make it better?" "Were you having trouble here?" "How do you feel about that?" Or if a student was dissatisfied, he might suggest "Maybe if you used a larger piece of paper and worked with crayons, you might like it better." He encouraged students to observe, compare, analyze, find problems, pose solutions, and test conjectures. Sarason (2002) reports that Schaefer declined to intrude into the students' development. He never hurried them and always treated them as serious artists developing their own aesthetic vision.

The results were spectacular. After several months the students not only made interesting drawings but used their designs to make rugs, placemats, and wall hangings. And these were inmates that no one thought were capable of learning let alone creating works of art. One shy, schizophrenic victim of child abuse produced such outstanding work that Schaefer arranged a public exhibition for the whole school. (For examples of these students' works see Henry Schaefer-Simmern, 1948.)

Schaefer attributed the success of the students to the power of his theory of artistic activity. What struck Sarason was the way Schaefer implemented the theory. The men became friends and worked together on Schaeffer's writings for 40 years. Sarason found Schaefer's violation of classroom norms fascinating. He gave minimal instruction, supplied materials and a purpose, asked few questions, and respected student attempts to express their aesthetic vision. Students responded with attention, thoughtfulness, persistence, and joy. Sarason called that *productive learning*.

Supporting students as they develop their own ideas and aesthetics led to learning. Or to paraphrase Papert interpreting Piaget, we learn by building our own view of the world. Schaefer helped students develop what was already in their brains. He thought that students needed to change and improve the knowledge structures they already possessed. To impose structures, however excellent, interrupts learning. Attempting to put ideas or images into student brains created resentment and boredom. Under duress, motivated students do find ways to develop their mental structures. To do so they hide their best efforts from their teachers. Sarason (2002) called that unproductive learning and summed up his observations in his memoir:

> In the course of spending scores of hours in classrooms, I was both appalled and puzzled by the passivity and conformity of the students and the lack of any air of excitement. In general the classrooms were pleasant, humane, even nurturing, but there were no sparks indicative of curiosity, propelling interests, eagerness, or sin of an active inner life. I did not then, as I do not now, expect students to display the degree of youthful piss and vinegar they display in venues outside of school, but I also did not expect them to be devoid of spontaneity and liveliness. There were exceptions, of course, there always are exceptions; they were very few in number but they had the compelling virtue of telling me that what I was ordinarily observing and concluding had validity, I was not 'making it up.' (p. 162)

Classrooms at all levels quash creativity and initiative. In the first grade my task was to rein in my curiosity. Instead, I fought the demands of school. I tried to find out what I needed to know. Stubbornness gave me an advantage. My skirmishes meant some misery but led to learning in an independent way. I don't mourn that angry boy. Throughout his years in the classroom as student and then as teacher he came to challenge these accepted routines and see them as opportunities for change.

Today we can see that Schaefer's view is similar to more recent theories in cognitive science that are central to this book. Briefly, the human brain, a product of eons of evolution, configures the ways we perceive the world. Innate structures enable us to identify and construct the patterns of objects and events. Brains select from the myriad inputs of light and sound waves, of touch and gravity to turn stimuli into symbols, which represent reality. The cells of our brains are somehow organized and function to create, use, and correct these representations or models of reality. Using their inborn rules brains can relate and transform these models. The brain is an agent of learning and an author of its experiences. This view departs from the persistent image of a brain that can be written on, sculpted, and instructed by experience.

These new cognitive theories are at odds with the idea of the mind as pliable, even blank, to be molded and inscribed by the events of experience, but those ideas have triumphed in education. Associated most frequently with E.L. Thorndike and B.F. Skinner, this seductive view of a mind reducible to laws of association implied that teaching is applied common sense and learning results from repetition and rewards. Connectionist brain folklore is embodied in the forms, architecture, schedules, vocabulary, daily practices, and even the uncomfortable seats of the classroom. Its pervasiveness makes it hard to grasp the implications of new insights.

We try to assimilate new ideas using old certainties. The results are bound to fail unless we work our way through the conflicts and paradoxes this produces. We need, in Piaget's terms, to accommodate those ideas by changing our understandings of how the mind works. But accommodation requires changing the way we think. That is difficult and even threatening. It confounds our comprehension of the mind and how it learns. I introduce these ideas here because they are the heartbeat of the book, explained and explored throughout the chapters that follow.

The model of teaching advocated here begins with questions—not the ones teachers ask students, but the ones students ask themselves. Teaching, then, is about creating environments and designing learning activities that cause students to ask questions—automatically. The questions come because what we know can't explain what we're confronting. Questions then become the bridge that connects what we don't know to what we realize we need to know, and I can explain that with a memorable example.

The Right Answer Is Always a Question

There was—an immaculate commode, chrome gleaming, white porcelain shining. The spout and handle of a drinking fountain sat in its bowl. A gag reflex wavered in the back of my throat. Disgusting.

"What's this?" a small voice barked at my side. I looked down to see a well-dressed boy. "It's a toilet, a crapper, right?" I nodded.

"But it has got a water fountain in it. Why do you suppose . . . ?" He smiled at me in a conspiratorial way. "Watch this." The boy stepped up to the exhibit, bent his head into the toilet, turned the handle and drank deeply.

"Did you see that?" he demanded.

"Yeah," I admitted but I didn't want to think about it. He watched me turn away. "I drank out of that potty like my dog. Hey, I bet you can't do that. I'll bet you a dollar."

"No, I don't want to bet." I smiled the way adults do when children aren't being appropriate.

"Yeah, you can't do it."

"Of course I can, but I don't want to take your money."

"I don't believe it. You just can't." By now a small crowd had gathered around us. I tried to move away but the boy grabbed my sleeve. "Why can't you?"

"It's disgusting sort of . . . " I answered.

"But it's shiny clean," he bent and took another. I couldn't say why I didn't want to drink from the crapper-fountain, but I definitely did not want to. Whenever he drank, I felt sick.

"Betcha can't" he repeated and there was a murmur from the small crowd. I stepped up to the commode bent down and turned the faucet to let the pure water arc into the bowl. Mouth inches from the spray I stopped. I stood up and tried to smile.

"You owe me a dollar," said the kid. Amid the snickers I paid and skulked off to the next exhibit.

That was a Frank Oppenheimer trick; use a social prop out of the context of its designated purpose. His exhibits get laughs, they shock, and set off questions about how stuff works. Why does the water stay together in a stream as it arcs instead of spraying everywhere? Or they raise questions about how the mind works. Why was I grossed out by a water fountain in a toilet? Or questions about public policies. Are public fountains sanitary? How did once cheap water become plastic bottled and more expensive than gasoline? Oppenheimer is the genius who created San Francisco's celebrated and widely copied museum of science, the *Exploratorium.*

When the doors open, children, adolescents, and adults charge or saunter across the space of several football fields. A conversational hum creates a symphony of questions punctuated by squeals of delight and wonder. Visitors watch, grab, and make things go. Guests smile or frown, stare or stroll, while the youngest or most curious twist, squeeze, push, or pound on the elegant but seemingly indestructible devices. If something intrigues them, they stop. If they get bored, they move on. All this takes place in a space under a banner that reads: "The right answer is always a question."

If you want to see questions promoted, this is heaven. And it seems simple until you look closely. The best way to generate student questions is to assign an interesting problem that you bet they won't understand and, as a wise colleague, Lisa Lenze, put it, "Leave it to them." The trouble is you must be willing to take the consequences. Maybe it isn't of interest to them and maybe they won't care. Oppenheimer accepted that challenge—perplex, intrigue, create quandaries—but always let them walk away; for puzzlement leads to inquiry and learning only if it is personal. As he wrote: "We don't 'rig' any of the exhibits; the exhibits do not show things artificially. The natural phenomena are there, and the visitors can ask questions of the exhibits, and the exhibits can then answer . . . because they behave according to nature."

His story is one of recovery from a career ending in failure. During the red scare investigations of the late 1940s, Oppenheimer admitted he had been a short-term member of the Communist party during his student days. He was fired from his faculty position in physics at the University of Minnesota. (The case was a sensation because of his famous older brother, J. Robert Oppenheimer.) He tried cattle ranching, but his passion for science led him to teach at rural Pagosa Springs High School in Colorado. The students were not curious about physics and Oppenheimer responded by building contraptions designed to capture their attention. He tried anything. For example, he took a class to the town junk yard and had them take apart the engines and appliances. Students got interested in how the stuff worked. Oppenheimer then used physics to explore the mysteries of television, internal combustion engines, washing machines and hair dryers. Students from his classes began to win statewide prizes with their research and experiments. Eventually he was recruited to teach at the University of Colorado. (To read a lively biography of this amazing man see Cole, 2009).

Established in 1969, his *Exploratorium* museum is a library of provocations designed to intrigue but not compel. Exhibit designers emphasize fundamental forces; stars are suns and nuclear explosions, planets and moons fall just as boulders and apples do, electricity produces magnetism and magnetism produces electricity and both combine to create light. Instead of textbook explanations patrons experience water waves, sound waves, light waves, and waves of fashion. Human perception connects the exhibits through artistic displays of optics, sounds, resonances, rotations, angular momentum, heat, gas, performing liquids, and all sorts of engines. The exhibits develop visitors' intuition of physical objects and processes. If an exhibit leaves too many observers befuddled, it is modified or thrown away. If one doesn't raise curiosity among many, it is redesigned. Oppenheimer insisted that the museum's exhibits be continuously adjusted to relax people about missing or not understanding something. He argued that "when people believe they are being listened to, they educate themselves."

Messing around enables students to make their own connections and test them. It often leads to an understanding that is so clear that, as Oppenheimer put it, students understand their understanding. Translation of those kinds of experiences into classrooms is a good goal of educational reform. We might do it if we could cease trying to work around traditional teaching methods like interrogating questions, lectures and forcing problems on students that we know they don't care about. These teaching failures require us to change our assignments until they deliver student questions. Oppenheimer's *Exploratorium* demonstrates what is possible. It shows that we can design situations or microworlds that allow students to explore their curiosity and learn from their mistakes without tricks or coercion.

Should we teach students to ask better questions? That might make small improvements, but it's another work around that detracts from the pursuit of alternatives. One of our worst habits as teachers is to take on more and more of the work of learning and think we are becoming better (but exhausted). We keep conveying the message that learning is our job and not a student responsibility. We seem to think that if we do what we want students to do, like good monkeys they will do it too. But for the most part they do not. They retreat. No one wants to ask the questions that other people want them to ask. And we don't want teachers to ask questions for us any more than we want them to walk, talk, or think for us.

Oppenheimer demonstrated another approach—teaching as design and as a response to student curiosity. That may be the foundation of future schools, a school in which I might have flourished instead of floundered. I didn't do much better as a teacher than I did as student. I'll use the failures I encountered in more than half a century in classrooms as a student, a professor and a reformer to raise questions about what's considered common knowledge and wise practice. In my search for answers, I've found authors who illuminate our extensive ignorance of learning and teaching. They suggest that the way forward is to fail better in the provocative words of Samuel Becket, but the opportunities to learn from errors, mistakes and failures are explored in chapter 9 and we've got early teaching experiences to explore next.

References

Cole, K. C. (2009). *Something incredibly wonderful happens: Frank Oppenheimer and the world he made up*. Houghton, Mifflin, Harcourt.

Papert, S. (1980). *Mindstorms: Children, computers and powerful ideas*. Basic Books.

Paradise, R. (1998). What's different about learning in schools as compared to family and community settings. *Human Development 41*(4), 270–276.

Sarason, S. B. (2002). *Educational reform: A self-scrutinizing memoir.* Teachers College Press.

Schaefer-Simmern, H. (1948). *The unfolding of artistic activity, Its bases, processes and implications.* University of California Press.

Willingham, D. T. (2017). *Why don't students like school?* Jossey-Bass.

2

EARLY TEACHING EXPERIENCES IN COLLEGE

I remember the day I discovered that I wanted to teach. After a morning at the typewriter, I walked down the hill in Pacific Grove, California with a full head of words and a heart full of questions. After many pages, lots of rejections, a stint as a reporter, even with a hard-won English degree, I wasn't sure I was a writer. So far, my efforts had garnered meagre results—stacks of manuscripts, some completed, most not, and a collection of slips that said "no" in a variety of encouraging and insulting ways. My days ached with disappointment.

I turned into an overgrown lot. The ground was beaten by decades of children's feet in a once schoolyard now the campus of an "experimental" college. Under a live oak tree a few students lounged in bright shifts and shirts, with brown toes sandaled. Their ages ranged from teens to late 20s. I nodded to a few I knew from the local coffee shops. We hunkered in the sun-plaited shade waiting to be taught.

The instructor, from New York, had made films of sugarcane cutters in Castro's Cuba and written about the new revolution. He rushed to the group and announced, flourishing a paperback, the class will discuss Karl Mannheim's (1952) *Ideology and Utopia.* As I watched it looked more like a beating. The fiery speaker cudgeled the air with words like intelligentsia, perspective, and objective. The dead Mannheim was sliced and diced. The teacher boomed a couple of questions. "What is 'an essentially human perspective?' How do we achieve a synthesis out of a conflict of ideas?"

The faces seem enraptured, but they didn't answer. "Material interest drives ideas," the teacher proclaimed, "And what does that mean?" Silence washed the attentive faces as the impatient Aristotle strode among the students. "Has anyone read the book?" All mumbled affirmation. One tousled student said, "It's difficult to understand."

"You're right. You're right. Yes, because the problem is hard. We're in a war of ideas, beset by propaganda, drowned in television, how can we know what is true? If we don't know, how can we act with reason? How can we be free if we don't know how to act politically? Come on get with this! You are here as an experiment. You don't want to be indoctrinated."

"We can't know the truth," I ejaculated, "That's the whole point." He pounced at me waving his arms, "Someone has read the book," he grinned sardonically. Seeing that I was not of the class, "Who are you?" he demanded.

"Just visiting. Just interested," I nodded. The teacher turned away and prodded the students mercilessly. Dutifully they spat Mannheim words until one hit the phrase, "a watchman in the night." With joy, the instructor led an animated chorus bemoaning the pitch-black night and the struggle for something called a "total perspective." I inhaled the ideas, felt the sun on my back, and remembered my own past as a boy who told tales to children under a backyard elm. For a few moments then I was the talking center of the world. Now I watched the languid students with their eyes fixed on this teacher. It seemed like coming home.

It wasn't that I really liked this teacher. He was too eager to bully, too quick to seize ignorance. He was raising consciousness, preaching. But what I liked were his hot articulate sentences, the thrust of his questions and the way he created new connections and new questions about Mannheim's sociology of knowledge. It was hard not to jump in. I remember thinking I could do it better. Maybe I could do it well. I knew I could make it interesting. *I want to do this*, I thought. *I want to talk about ideas. I want to profess, argue, and riff on the best thoughts of the culture.* The thought of returning to my lonely typewriter and overflowing ashtray repelled me. As I felt the orphaned dollar bills in my pocket, I wondered if I could make a living doing this.

Learning to Teach: Awkward Beginnings

I started teaching in January of 1965 when the San Francisco Art Institute hired me to teach an introduction to political science for a trial semester. I began knowing that I'd been a student who'd fought teachers and their attempts to make me learn from grade school through college. Now it was my turn to teach. I took it as a dare. Convinced that boredom killed learning, I would teach to incite curiosity.

I was nervous, but I prepared what I thought was a brilliant introduction to political science. If humans are political animals, then survival is served by politics. What better way to think about that than to present what we've learned about the social structures of monkeys, chimpanzees, and baboons.

I began by contrasting the bands of anarchistic howler monkeys with the more patriarchal baboon troops.

I looked up—the faces were blank and hostile. I tried to slow down, lower my voice, step away from the podium and gesture. Panic drove my words faster. I stared at a deep crack in the plaster on the far wall. My voice rose loudly and spoke so rapidly the words might as well have been Latin. I arrived at the last page of my notes. Stunned, I discovered I'd delivered my hour lecture in 20 minutes.

I mumbled something about the readings for next week and croaked: "Class dismissed." The students ambled out, careful not to look at me. Grabbing my new briefcase, I ran out the door and stumbled down the street. Terror strangled my thoughts. I meditated on the meaning of "abject." On that first day I didn't just strikeout, I waved my bat wildly and fell across home plate.

I went over my notes. A biological approach was (at the time) rare; it should have grabbed attention. My closely reasoned lecture demonstrated my expertise. Well researched, but speculative, it introduced the abstractions of political thought—power, control, cooperation, obedience, dissent—from an amusing perspective. Why didn't it work? I'd made a typical teacher mistake. I presented conclusions to novices who needed something rougher, more particular, and less polished that they could grasp and work on. I failed miserably to understand the basic task of a teacher.

I had to give the students hand holds onto or pathways into the subject. I had to seduce. Luckily the next syllabus topic was an analysis of Herbert Marcuse's (1966) *Eros and Civilization*. Sex might do it. Polymorphous perversity might capture the students' interest. I prepared an entertainment, part stand-up comedy, part Freudian erudition, and part incendiary critique of the pleasure principle. It couldn't miss and I slept well the night before.

Nervously casual, I begin laying out Freud's views of sexuality. Students were on the edge of their tablet desks as I plunged into the taboos of Oedipus. I said the word "erogenous" and a hand shot up. I wanted to cheer, but instead said, "Yes, you have a question?"

"Are you one of those guys who thinks everyone wants to sleep with their mother? Do you want to sleep with your mother?" It was a female student in a long, flowing, wine-colored dress topped with a flamboyant hat.

"It's more complicated," I began.

"That's what teachers always say. You raised the issue. Give me a straight answer," she demanded.

The class responded. Some shouted down my interlocutor and some demanded an answer. Students yelled at each other and at me.

"You're showing off."

"Let him talk!"

"What kind of a poli sci teacher talks about monkeys?"

I heard the questioner shout, "Maybe you're nuts, Teach."

I needed to regain some control. "One at a time!" I tried to direct the flow of questions, assertions, and outrageous jokes on perversity, postindustrial society, pop culture, Marshall McLuhan, incest, patriarchy, and penis envy. I never finished my lecture. "This was fun," someone said, as the class ran overtime. When I described the events to my wife that night, she said, "You're going to get fired."

Was that class success or disaster? I'd connected, but I'd lost control. The students were interested in ideas; even passionate once they got started. The outcome was enthusiastic noise. I underestimated them; indeed, I didn't know them and set out to learn about them. In the weeks ahead I discovered that art students were, on average; smarter, older, more opinionated, and less civil. They paid tuition to paint, sculpt, design, and photograph—not to explore humanities and sciences. I was on trial as a teacher. Did I look and act like a teacher? Was I enthusiastic, understandable, and sympathetic? But also, was I knowledgeable? And in the creative culture of the institute, did I astonish in the classroom?

The third week was Plato's *Republic.* My preliminary notes critiqued Plato's utopia as romantic totalitarianism. That wasn't going to work. The lecture had to be relevant and explosive and so I decided to focus on Plato's argument that an ideal world would contain no artistic representations that threatened to pervert and corrupt the citizenry. There could be no poets in the *Republic,* only copywriters imitating the speech of decent people. Painters and sculptors could only be employed to depict people doing civically virtuous things. After presenting Plato's position, I would ask for the students' responses—only this time I would insist on arguments: Opinions had to be backed with reasons, examples, or evidence.

I began class with a lecture on Plato's arguments. When a hand went up or a face turned angry, I asked them to wait until Plato's case was clear. A few students dozed off but one seated far in the back of the class beamed every time I said, "Plato." This encouraged me. "Plato claimed," I would say, and he would nod agreement or pump his fist. What a discussion this would be. I hurried to the end and opened the gates to debate. The students trashed Plato as a pettifogging, puritanical pedant. "Name-calling won't do," I asserted. "Tell me what's wrong with his argument; his reasons." Order emerged as students attacked the assumption that artists only copy appearances. "What about Picasso?" Others countered Plato with examples of beautiful paintings and statues. "There's Botticelli." The lone Platonist sat smiling. As the students filed out, I walked back to him.

"And when did you develop a passion for Plato?" I asked.

"In kindergarten," he answered, "Play-Doh was my favorite stuff. It's why I want to be an artist to mold shapes and colors. Man, that was a neat discussion of Play-Doh. Great class."

The semester promised disaster if I couldn't figure this out. I was splashing alone in waters of ignorance, putting on a show and maybe (I hoped) promoting some learning. Some things worked, like insisting on arguments instead of assertions. But that brought new problems. Some students thought arguments meant insults. Some argued in the crudest manner. Onward I threw myself propelled by pride and instinct to plunge through Machiavelli, Hobbes, Kant, the Federalist Papers, and Marx. I knew nothing of pedagogy and my mistakes were multiple.

Even so, I landed the job based on an invited talk about the Free Speech Movement at Berkeley and the recommendation of Richard Miller. Miller, a Berkeley PhD in history, was an iconoclastic lecturer considered the best humanities teacher at the Institute. My model and mentor, he gave terse advice: "Don't bore or be pompous, talk to students directly as in a conversation, and tell interesting stories." That was my compass. Apparently, there were no standards for selecting candidates for teaching. It seemed anyone could teach. "Look, you are articulate. You can deliver a good talk. Now just use your imagination," Miller advised.

Asking graduate school colleagues produced few useful answers. Some said the art of teaching was a gift; you have it or you don't. Younger faculty said teaching sucked up the energy needed for research and offered advice on how to control its harm: Always schedule classes for late afternoons, save the mornings for writing and thinking, use standard textbooks, develop course outlines and lecture notes that can be reused every year, lighten your teaching "load" with seminars and graduate courses, and most of all, do as little of it as you can get away with. Needless to say, from my first teaching experiences I learned little.

Learning to Teach: The Trial and Error Method

Initially I taught as I'd been taught. I presented, explained, and then questioned. It was the same pattern that had alienated me as a student, but I did it with a great and earnest energy and used that to disguise my anxieties. Over time I discovered that the students were more like me, the person, than me, the struggling teacher. I found myself wanting to treat them how I wished I'd been treated as a student, to know what interested them, what bothered them, what they loved and hated, and most of all what they wanted to learn and who did they want to become? To get personal with them I had to let them know my interests and concerns. In a frightening sense, I had to be myself. Getting personal, I soon learned, meant becoming a friend. Of course, that didn't fit the role of a teacher as I had observed it. I had to look and act like a teacher at the same time I was revealing my personhood. I struggled with how to reconcile these conflicting impulses.

I ended up taking the side of the students; listening to them, watching them, and changing assignments and activities to activate them. In the classroom I admitted when I didn't know something or had my doubts. I came to work early and hung out in the student cafeteria. I stayed after class to drink coffee in the courtyard. It became clear that these students learned in studios where they drew, chiseled, slathered, and printed—everything was hands on. They learned to create their art by doing art. Could I do that in the classroom? If I stopped a lecture after 20 minutes and gave them a break, would they return and discuss what I had said? They did, and more of them took part in the discussion.

I was learning to teach by trial and error. I took every opportunity to surprise students and observe the results. Since students didn't think my lecture on monkey behavior provided insights into the nature of politics, I took them to the San Francisco Zoo. We went to Monkey Island where a large troop of black-handed spider monkeys roamed a concrete island dominated by fake grey mountains and surrounded by a wide odiferous moat.

"Observe the monkeys," I instructed, "Write down anything that might be related to politics."

The students obeyed, sort of. Some began sketching. Others exchanged gossip. Half a dozen monkeys moved toward us to beg. Other monkeys just watched, their long black tails grasping tree limbs or curling around their companions. Most ignored us. The young ones leapt, chased, and wrestled; the females fed their infants; male adults groomed each other. Adult females without infants disappeared into grottos. In the seeming chaos I could spot the colony's organization—the dominant male group, the female association, scattered juveniles, and romping youngsters. The students did not see the structure. "What is it you want us to see?"

"Look for what's going on from a political perspective," I explained.

A fight broke out on the island. A raging male chased a female across the rocks. All six mature males joined in. The female ran off. Triumphant, the aggressor joined his brothers in quietly grooming each other.

"Was that politics?" a student asked.

"Why do you think it might be?"

"It was violence, fighting, showing off, males dominating, female victims."

"Okay, watch the monkeys now and think about how they are organized. On impulse, I added. "Write two descriptive sentences about the group structure. Share your sentences with a partner. Pick out the most important observation and report that back to the class."

Students shifted and paired. Words, laughs, and then arguments buzzed in the afternoon sun. They were starting to see the politics of Monkey Island—the strict segregation of genders, the cluster of mothers and potential mothers, the marginal gang of juvenile males, and the ruling senate of mature males. And then came the questions I was waiting for.

"Why did the female run away? Why didn't she fight?, she was just as big. Why did the other males get into it? Why didn't the females protect her?"

And then came the best question, "This can't be the way they are organized in the wild, can it?"

After a number of field trips, I figured out that one of the reasons they work is because they bring classes together and make instructors more human. I could see that deviating from standard teaching practice made things more interesting, but I didn't understand why. I knew it was risky, that quantifying what, if anything, the students had learned would be difficult, if not impossible. Still, I pressed on trying anything that would get the students arguing, deciding, and thinking.

As the semester's end neared, the course and those I now called "my students" became sources of hectic pleasure. I enjoyed their company, their sarcasm, and their spirited good will. Come spring, the brown California hills burst green and bloomed with wildflowers and poppies. The institute hired me half time for the fall. On top of that, the Political Science Department at Berkeley awarded me a graduate fellowship.

Learning to Teach: Starting to Question

At the beginning of a teaching career, you don't question the infrastructure of teaching—its hallowed practices, traditions, and biases are accepted without thought or recognition. I assigned essays and guided discussion. It was amazingly easy to mark student essays with "C"s "B"s, or "A"s. I didn't consider whether the assignment had any connection to learning or whether the assigned grade had much meaning. I guided discussions with questions, even though on the other end of the technique I clammed up, insulted that teachers would assault me with fake, "Guess what I am thinking?" interrogations.

I also plunged into a deadening activity that I would pursue for the next 35 years. I prepared quizzes and exams—the very kind I had once despised.

As a student, I had hated questions that only tested whether I had read something, or whether I could repeat what the teacher had said. I wanted to demonstrate my knowledge creatively and to show that I could do something with the information I'd learned. But teachers were expected to give exams and so I did.

Like many new professors flailing through those first semesters, I did what everyone else did. Despite how courses were structured, I never thought to ask whether that was a structure that promoted learning or possibly impaired it. It never crossed my mind that courses might have been structured for their convenience, good for keeping records, allocating space, and controlling faculty time. It was years before I realized that courses don't give teachers enough time to plan, prepare, and conduct a class session and they don't give students enough time to practice under supervision and sustain improvements.

I did learn how to compose a presentation that would hold students' attention and stimulate their interest. Leading several seminars a day on the same subject gave me plenty of opportunities to practice and learn from my mistakes. I might start in the morning by leading a rambling discussion of Max Weber's analysis of bureaucracy. On break I would review the stumbles and refine my expectations. By the third time I could sail the class through Weber's turgid prose to a discussion of his "iron cage" that touched students personally.

At the Art Institute, I had wide latitude to experiment. Because in an art school, the teaching of social science only draws attention from the administration when there are complaints, I could do whatever I wanted as long as my students were enthusiastic and my distinguished art colleagues weren't offended.

Even so, questions fluttered like bats in my mental attic. Are they learning? What did they learn? How could they improve? But those questions stayed in the shadows. I survived by accepting the infrastructure that would come to imprison my teaching life. The questions that later dominated my thinking remained unexplored. I assumed the only way to educate students was with courses, content-heavy lectures, and by grading. By not questioning, I saw teaching and learning from inside a set of blinders.

After many years of trying, failing, and learning, I know things about teaching now that I didn't, indeed couldn't know when I started. Hindsight makes me feel like I was an idiot. But the details of how my early teaching experiences felt are vivid. I can't write about them without guilt. Why didn't I see or act? Why did I ignore failure? Why did I leap at conclusions beyond my understanding and improvise solutions to problems I barely understood? I suspect I was neither as stupid nor as smart as I remember. My performance earned an "A" for persistence, but much lower marks for everything else. Most embarrassing were my periodic bouts of almost delusional overconfidence.

My first teaching experiences happened at a unique institution and that certainly helped shape my first teaching attempts, but much of what I experienced is typical of beginning college teachers. We begin without or with very little training. We teach as we were taught and fluctuate between anxiety, awkwardness, and failure on the one hand, and overconfidence on the other hand. We're without supervision and little or no assistance from colleagues. New teachers focus on teaching, assuming learning flows from it as an all but automatic outcome. But is it?

Learning to Teach: What I Finally Discovered

No one talked about learning. Either students learned or they didn't. Were we afraid to discuss it? Was it too simple or maybe the opposite, too mysterious to fathom? But if doctors could not treat illness without understanding human biology, and lawyers could not practice if they didn't know the laws, then how could I teach without out knowing how people learned? A library rat since the third grade, when puzzled I browsed the stacks and scavenged used bookstores. Anywhere I could find books I expected enlightenment. And there it was. Small and grey with fluorescent letters the book announced: *Doubt and Certainty in Science: A Biologist's Reflections on the Brain.* The author was one John Zachary Young (1960), a zoologist who had spent his life studying the neurons of the giant squid.

So profoundly did that book shake and then shape the way I thought about teaching and learning that it is difficult now to recreate its impact. Young described learning as doubt—the search for new information and perspectives when current assumptions fail. Knowledge developed through cycles of doubt and certainty. Doubt was the search for alternatives; sorting through and selecting makeshift ways to see, act and think about what wasn't making sense. Certainty was what survived—what remained after the trials and criticism—and it's what we call knowledge.

Young's views made me doubt what I thought I understood about teaching. My task was not just polishing and presenting already established knowledge. It was to question what we think of as models, create doubt, so that other explanations could be tested and explored until they became a new level of certainty, certainty that raised questions, and caused doubt. The way knowledge moves forward is a cycle that starts and ends with questions. I'm exploring questions in detail in an upcoming chapter.

Doubt, wrote Young, is the first step in learning. I was skipping that step and pouring wisdom into the students. But if learning begins with doubt and questions, then the brain isn't a recording device. The idea that brains represented reality, that is, made models of it or created stories about it, but did not record, it raised a whole slew of questions for me. If our brains conjure the knowledge which helps us live, then teaching could not be the telling of wisdom, but that's what happens in school. Teachers present and reinforce what is already known. Either this brain scientist was wrong, or schools have failed miserably.

If he was right, then learning must be done by the learner and so, in a classroom where students are doing the learning, then what's the function of the teacher? Young gave me some ideas. First, I had to understand the students—their ways of thinking and their certainties. What was already in their brains? Student interests, resistance, even chatter became something to investigate. But that went against classroom culture. Why would a teacher listen to those who need to be taught? That would be pandering, pampering and not doing my job.

I was a student in graduate courses when I discovered Young and started asking these questions. In my graduate courses my views were frequently ignored, and my ideas disparaged. I was experiencing the same failings in graduate education—lectures that induced sleep, professor-dominated discussions, disdain for student questions. Even so, graduate school still offered a better learning atmosphere than I experienced previously. Classes met less frequently, and independent work was required and appreciated. Although some professors were gurus encouraging clones, others were more like senior colleagues. In some courses, what I learned on my own got attention, encouragement, and criticism.

Based on Young and my experiences in graduate school I developed a new approach for my teaching, what I called "action to knowledge." Implementing it immediately raised problems. First, I had to get the content I was supposed to teach (read transmit) into forms that would motivate student action. That is, the students had to get involved with the content. They had to care about it, be interested in it. Second, I had to set up assignments that demanded thinking, and third, I had to find ways that students could show what they had learned in a way that could be evaluated. My approach depended on knowing what students knew and connecting to that. I needed to know what Young called their "models of reality"—that is, how they thought about, organized, and used their knowledge. My first discovery was that students knew more than I or they reckoned. Their brains were full and that offered obstacles as well as opportunities.

This radical change in my approach to teaching took place in those tumultuous years dominated by the Vietnam War, student protest, and race riots, as well as the first heart transplants and men on the moon. Daily life threatened to explode. Families, friends, and colleagues found themselves on hostile sides of deep cracks in the culture. Any conversation, opinion, or gesture could become a fight. I didn't want to dampen student passions, but I did want them to listen, seek common ground, sift evidence, and create arguments.

The students invented one of the techniques that became important in advancing the goals of my approach. We called it sociodrama. During one of the periodic Bay Area university strikes, I invited a street theatre group to perform for a seminar section on bureaucracy. After a warm-up, the players assigned students parts in a college insurrection farce. Students played policemen, professors, trustees, a governor, a college president, and a range of outraged, apathetic, or reactionary citizens. So entranced did we become that the class ran over for an additional hour. Students' abilities to enact characters they said they disliked showed that they understood the values and perspectives of people from all walks of life. They also understood the constraints of professions, positions, race, and religion. Each had an elaborate model of American society in their minds. Through this approach they were learning political science but in whole different way.

At Christmas, the class concluded with one last sociodrama. At the door each student picked up a card that described a secret persona that they had to enact. Males were assigned female roles, black students assigned white and Asian roles, white students became black militants, and students aged to be septuagenarians. Of course, I was assigned to be a "genius" artist flunking out of school. Amid snacks celebrating the end of the course we played our roles in student-contrived scenarios—occupants in a bus, customers in a supermarket, inmates of a drunk tank, tourists at the Palace of the Legion of Honor, Art Institute Trustees at board meetings, public officials defending the war, and through it all students revealed that they knew a great deal about the social structures, the power struggles, the status games, and the humiliations of the world. I'd never before been able to teach students this much political science.

These sociodramas demanded a truthfulness that was at once painful and exhilarating. They couldn't happen without trust. And I found you cannot demand trust; you must cultivate it and hope it grows. It started with me. I had to trust the students, first. Moderating, as if I secretly knew the answers, didn't work. I had to put my views and opinions on the line and take criticism and dissent from students just as they took mine. It was an approach that made us partners in learning.

Sometimes there was more drama than I'd bargained for. A Renaissance seminar heated up over a discussion of the relationship of artists to tyrants. Some believed that the Church and usurpers like the Medici corrupted artists into producing propaganda. Their opponents argued that the artist exploited the resources of church and state to develop critical visions of human freedom. Voices rose, fists clenched. Anger was everywhere in the room. I shouted, "Sit down. Take a deep breath. Let's sit at the table and get back to the discussion." It worked. Voices lowered, and the raucous views advanced to arguments. No one wanted, least of all me, the class to stop. The words became smaller, the silent spaces larger until we sat quietly. I had to break the spell. "Once we feel safe together we can disagree about ideas."

For these art students, normal classrooms were dull compared with bustling studios of paint, clay, and nude models. They complained of drowsiness and begged to go outside. We tried different venues. We held class in empty studios, in the library, by the Marina, at Ocean Beach, by the Golden Gate Bridge, at Bay wharves, in Golden Gate Park, on Angel Island, at street corners, in abandoned patios, and on the Institute's roof. The changes delighted, their settings rich with beauty, and did not make concentration more difficult as I had supposed. I'd never thought about what kinds of environments promote learning. I couldn't believe how effectively these improvised classrooms constrained my habit of talking too much. They made it impossible to lecture.

Again and again I confronted questions about the approach. I could see students were learning, but were they learning what I was supposed to be teaching? I could see improvements in intellectual skills. They read assignments to gain ammunition for our weekly exchanges. They developed their ability to construct arguments and detect crap. But many activities uncovered garbage dumps of ignorance, clichés, and slogans. Students could enact a simulation of a *coup d'état* and still not understand the different powers of a president or a Supreme Court justice. They would design a democratic community and still curtail speech. As my tenure wore on I started having the same students in other courses I taught. That was often dismaying. They remembered so little of what I thought they had learned and were not using the skills I assumed they'd mastered.

I made mistakes—some of them serious. The sociodrama approach was so powerful that I ignored the possibilities for harm. There was an exhilarating session on fascism and its roots in the 20th century. To get the students to experience the intimidation and the exultation of mass hysteria, we organized the classroom as a Nazi party rally with me parading up and down the seminar table shouting orders and insults; extolling and humiliating; gesticulating in the grandest Hitler manner. Pleased with my performance I was shocked the next day when a large student delegation showed up at my office. "We want to talk to you about class yesterday"

"Yes, didn't that go well?"

"No, it didn't. It made us feel awful. And ashamed."

"Well, yes, that was the point."

"We get the point, but we don't think you should have manipulated and humiliated us."

Queasy, I grabbed for the nearest straw. "Well, some of the class must have thought it was good. I see less than half of you. Maybe there was . . ."

"Oh, yeah they were right. They said not to come. They said it wouldn't make any difference—you were just going to do your thing and wouldn't listen."

All pedagogy is poisonous, wrote Alice Miller (1997). Like a useful drug it can harm in excess. Teachers poke into brains trying to make learning happen. They push to bring out the best in students. But poking can hurt and damage. Pushing can call out some of our darkest desires for control. Students seem to invite shaping. They seem to want help. As a result, some of the architecture and practices of the classroom undermine both students' autonomy and instructors' caution. The intimacy of the classroom demands boundaries. I apologized then and in the next session to the entire class. They accepted.

I wasn't going to make scholars or social scientists out of these students. I wasn't going to lay out cheat sheets of Western culture for them to carry around in their back pockets and quote at cocktail parties. What I might do was kindle their desire to learn and keep on learning. Wanting to learn reaches beyond the classroom and the specific focus of a discipline. It prepares students to take on future problems that are impossible to know in the present.

Much about my "action to knowledge" approach confused me. Everything in my years as a student and now as a teacher said my goal should be to transmit the values, perspectives, knowledge, and wisdom of the past. Yet, I lived in an age of science where, as Young noted, the goal was to doubt the most secure and sacred of ideas. Didn't I have an obligation to not only foster doubt but to ensure that certainty took its place? I wasn't sure. My best days and best achievements, however, were when I obeyed Yeats and lit fires instead of filling buckets.

It's time to sum up. After this rollicking apprenticeship, colleagues concluded I was a natural teacher. Although I appreciated their encouragement, I thought they were wrong. Smarting from early failures, I felt I was still far from being a good teacher. Colleagues also warned that my interests in teaching would ruin my career. I suppose it did. But it surely made my academic life thought-provoking and happy. Stymied by culture, colleagues, and administrators, and overwhelmed by failures, I burnt out many times. But approaching learning as a research project renewed me. It made teaching an exciting quest. Facing my ignorance made me an optimist.

References

Mannheim, K. (1952). *Ideology and utopia.* Routledge.

Marcuse, H. (1966). *Eros and civilization: A philosophical inquiry into Freud.* Beacon Press.

Miller, A. (1997). *The drama of the gifted child: The search for the true self.* Basic Books.

Young, J. Z. (1960). *Doubt and certainty in science: A biologist's reflections on the brain.* Oxford University Press.

3

IT'S TIME TO PUT LECTURES ON THE SHELF

I'd like to start with how I experienced lectures. No matter how boring and dull the classes in primary grades through high school, I could always conjure a pastime to keep myself amused. Daydreams, clandestine war games fought on paper, drawings, doodles, the molding of crayons into miniature cannons, and surreptitious reading material got me through.

Only when I got to college did the dullness of large lectures put me to sleep. When I tried to focus on the lecture eyes would droop, the world would fade, and the droning voice would become a lullaby. I tried to take notes, chatted quietly with a student seated nearby, but nodding off was still a problem. Finally, I hit upon the simple solution of attending every third class. Trying to figure out what was going on kept me awake and engaged.

Here is a secret I don't often admit: I screwed up my Ivy League freshman year. I was ill-prepared, eager but antagonistic. The lectures shocked me. How could I learn by listening to mere talk and more talk? If I listened carefully, I forgot to take notes. If I took careful notes I missed large gaps of the lecture. Introductory physics was at 9 a.m. and a good half mile from my morning job in a college dining hall where I earned my scholarship. After a jog to make the class I watched a professor work spider-like to fill the blackboard with formulas. His running explanations were mostly addressed to the board. I tried to write down the formulas, but I focused on words. "Vector" I would hear and "vector" I would write followed by my best imitation of the diagrams and symbols chalked on the board. It was no use. At the end of the first week, I failed the quiz and I panicked. My advisor helped me drop the course and replace it with geology in the afternoon.

The geology lecture hall was larger than my hometown's movie theater. The lecturer was a tall, military-looking paleontologist and renowned author of the hefty textbook. His talk was punctuated by slides of minerals, fossils, boulders, outcrops, glaciers, volcanoes, lava, and dinosaurs. Truthfully, they weren't that interesting. For the most part, the problem was that I couldn't understand what he said. I just didn't know the words—aquicludes, quaternary, stratigraphy, trilobites, Mesozoic, Devonian, sediment, glaciation, carboniferous, tectonic, carbonate—the list went on. This expert bombardment of terms, facts, and timelines of worlds long dead and disasters long forgotten buried me in the rubble.

In desperation I read the textbook like a novel. The first half was physical geology—how the earth got the way it is. The second half was paleontology—how evolution shaped life on earth. As I read the textbook through the second of three times, I began to understand the professor's language. Not like a vocabulary list but as elements in a new way of looking at the world. Only then did I start taking a few notes on select topics likely to show up on exams. I came to class loaded with unspoken questions and the lectures answered many of them. The course became a delight. I posted the highest score on the massive multiple-choice final exam. It was, of course, an inventory of the facts and stories in the textbook and lectures. It basically asked did you read and hear and can you remember?"

I could easily remember the material, but I had not memorized it. I made sense of the material in ways that related to my interest and life. Fascinated by Alfred Sherwood Romer's (1971) rule that evolutionary changes enabled creatures to continue their old ways of life instead of adapting to new ones, I identified with transition species like the early stegocephalia whose ancestors survived by flopping from one drying water hole to another under drought conditions. I read paleontology as a saga of heroic organisms that struggled to stay the same and so became revolutionaries. Of course, that's a personal fantasy not a scientific view, but it propelled me into the theory of evolution. I could see and feel desperate semi fish using their fins to wriggle across mud flats. This sensitized me to patterns in the fossil record. It was my form of deliberate practice: to pose questions about what I didn't understand and seek answers until I did. I knew better than to discuss my unusual approach with the professor, but it worked so I kept my mouth shut.

Now my philosophy course that started with readings from Descartes' meditations was a different story. Not only could I not understand the lectures, I couldn't make sense of text. I wrestled with every sentence. Descartes said our senses mislead so we can't trust them. I couldn't believe that. When I was a child, my father insisted that if you lied no one would ever believe you. I discovered that wasn't true. The adults around me lied regularly but I still trusted them. I learned through experience when to question, (but never out loud) their pronouncements. Some of those around me exaggerated, some avoided conflict, some were overly polite and some thought children liked lies about Santa Claus, Easter bunnies, and the Sandman. Faced with a short paper due the following week in philosophy, I wrote an attack on Descartes based on my experience. Two things happened. First, I got an unexpected "80" and second, the professor polished my argument and presented it (without attribution) in his next lecture as a "common-sense" retort to Descartes.

Emboldened, I tore into whatever philosopher we were reading—Plato, Dewey, or Russell—it didn't matter; I just criticized. Each paper was a polemic—blustery and sarcastic. Luckily the distinguished professor, who also led my recitation section, found me amusing. His counter critiques sharpened my skills, and I began to understand the weird philosophical way of looking at things. Philosophy is more a skill then the organization of facts and principles. It is a form of creating and criticizing abstract models. Since I didn't know how to create the models, I tore into the ones the assigned texts presented. But in doing so I began to feel my way into my own understanding of philosophy. I became a crude street corner philosopher. Of course, I was, in the eyes of real philosophers, silly and crude to be mocked like Thrasymachus.

I wasn't able to figure out ways to avoid lectures in all my courses. Some, like introductory astronomy, were just plug and chug, memorizing, and calculating. Some interminably dull. In these courses I ignored understanding and I followed the lead of my fellow students; cram the night before the tests and hope for the best.

Can we just dismiss what I did as tricks to pass courses? Initially, that was how I thought of them. But there was something more at work. The gothic learning cathedrals promised me that I could achieve knowledge, learn to think, to imagine and to polish my work into something public and useful. I wanted to become an expert, a scholar, or an artist—someone with the knowledge and information to make a difference. I would not only read the great thinkers and answer questions about them, I would be able to wear them like enchanted spectacles to see the world differently and better. I would someday write like Eliot, think like Russell, solve mysteries like Darwin, or create them like Galileo. I desired to enter the enlightened temple of knowledge and not stand taking notes at the doorway.

Between my need to know and understand, and the need to memorize and regurgitate on demand, I struggled. Lectures not only bored, they repelled. I wanted to know how to be a knowledgeable intellectual, but what they seemed to teach was how to repeat the words and rules. The contradiction I saw between the conscious questioning and guessing of scientists, mathematicians, and poets, and the drab orthodoxy of the classroom cheated me. I wanted to be like the best lecturers that I encountered. But the classroom demanded fidelity, certainty, conformity. It proclaimed that knowledge would result from following the rules. To get to the world I wanted to join I knew that I had to think my way in.

A lab rat pressing levers and running dingy corridors was not what I wanted. I hated the hoop jumping and the parroting. I could not fit and would not adapt. In the language of the university, I was not making the grade. Indeed, I was often absent, fleeing the lecture halls for my old refuge, the library. To succeed at what seemed a charade meant a betrayal of me. But to refuse to succeed betrayed my family and sponsors. I stopped caring and with that I was lost indeed. I tried to escape by trying out for the student newspaper. I partied. I disparaged the efforts of others and hid behind a vicious wit. The forced hypocrisy of daily survival brought pain. I saw enemies everywhere, not realizing I was my own worst enemy.

After making the dean's list the first semester my grade point average for the year fell to 1.7. The university did not renew my scholarship and essentially expelled me to "take responsibility for your actions" as my advisor told me. "When you mature you can be reinstated." And so ended my Ivy League career.

The Evidence Against Lectures

I now know that a great deal of evidence has been amassed showing that lectures don't work. They're a poor way to communicate information, knowledge, or even enthusiasm. They put students to sleep and promote illusions of knowledge. Their failure points to faulty assumptions about brains, learning, and teaching. Although, as performances by orators, actors, and stand-up comedians, lectures may be entertaining, even compelling, one thing they seldom do, if ever, is teach.

Over the years many professors have recorded their dismal experiences with lectures. In the 1950s, a pioneer in physics education reform, Arnold Arons (1997) came to realize that students remembered nothing from his lectures and demonstrations. Another physics professor, Joe Redish, hired a graduate student to grab students as they left his wonderful lectures and ask: "What was the lecture you just heard about?" The students' answers were disturbingly vague. Eric Mazur taught a popular introductory physics course at Harvard in the 1980s. When he read that other physics professors found their lectures in introductory physics course didn't change student understanding, he doubted that applied to his course. He asked his students simple questions about Newtonian mechanics and found they were unable to answer. Still in disbelief, Mazur interviewed more than 100 students, one-on-one, only to confirm their conceptual problems. His students were bright. They could solve quantitative problems. But he found that they memorized recipes for solving them without understanding the underlying ideas (Mazur 2009).

The physics Nobel Laureate, Carl Wieman tried to measure the results of his "brilliantly clear explanations." He offered a nonobvious fact in a lecture, supported it with an illustration, and then quizzed students 15 minutes later. Only 10% remembered the fact. He repeated the experiment at a colloquium for physics faculty and graduate students and got about the same result. In all of these cases, little understanding of physics was retained from the best lectures. Weiman (2017) reported that new physics graduates, who entered his lab after 17 years of school and high grades, still didn't grasp the fundamental ideas of physics.

Wilbert McKeachie (1986), an acclaimed educational psychologist who not only summarized the research, but did a lot of it, notes lectures can transfer information as effectively as discussion methods but they are inferior in terms of what students retain, can apply in other situations, or use in problem solving. They don't encourage thinking, attitude change, or motivate learning as well as discussions do and they encourage student passivity. He believes that "one of the greatest barriers to effective lecturing is the feeling that one must cover the material at all costs" (p. 81). Instead of exclusively focusing on the content, McKeachie proposes that lectures involve analyzing materials, formulating problems, developing hypotheses, bringing evidence to bear, criticizing and evaluating alternative solutions. What he doesn't explain is how lectures that showcase these skills enable students to develop the same skills. Watching some expert do an analysis is no more helpful than watching your personal trainer flex her biceps. You will get a vague idea of what you want to accomplish, but no notion of the trials and efforts needed. Or, to use another example, lectures are like watching football on television. After a while you can talk football but without the knowledge needed to play the game.

I could fill the rest of this chapter with research evidence collected in many fields all documenting what students don't learn and can't do after listening to lectures. We have over 7 decades of research showing that lectures result in woefully poor understanding. Lectures are as good, but no better than audio tapes, movies, videos, or books for transmitting information, not effective for promoting student thinking. Furthermore, they fail to change student attitudes toward the subject matter or the values of disciplines. Lectures are greatly inferior to "nondirected" reading, defined as reading that students choose out of curiosity and interest (Bligh, 2000.)

Even So, I Lectured

I did return to college and earned undergraduate and graduate degrees. After my first teaching experiences at the Art Institute, I moved to teach at a more traditional university. I'd been there teaching for a decade. My hair was thinner and darker, my freckles buried in a reddish beard and my eyes looked from behind aviator glasses. More rotund than muscled, I strutted with tenure. I was elated, felt light on my feet. There was less weight on my mind and less fear in my gut. Sociodramas wouldn't have helped my case for tenure, nor would they have worked well for these younger undergraduates. The 70s were long gone and I was doing what my colleagues did—I lectured.

Worse than that, I have to admit I liked to lecture, to perform. I liked to prepare lectures; the search for astonishments, the clarification of complex ideas, and the creation of stories to illustrate abstract principles. From the beginnings of my teaching the work on lectures was an important source of my own education. It gave me an impetus to read, strategically asking questions of the text: Is this the main point, will students understand this, would this help someone think through the problem, what's the weakest link in the argument? Always I sought big explanations and expansive ideas.

I liked to walk into a crowded room, write an outrageous proclamation on the board and face the students, eager to show them the statement was not all that wrong, might be right, and was wonderful to tear apart. To uncover clues to our hidden ignorance delighted me. I liked to provoke and entertain. Indeed. I was sometimes a ribald show-off garnering students' laughs and sometimes eliciting wonderful questions. On good days I could demonstrate how to analyze a problem or take apart a famous argument.

Not all days were good, though. The students could be quiet, hostile—I suspected a student like I had been might be lurking in the classroom. That motivated me to work on improving my lectures. When I taught courses for a second or third time, I rewrote my lecture notes, polished phrases, concocted new stories, and developed other examples. I worked hard to get better. Recording the lectures, I listened for dead moments, murky statements, and pompous clichés and tried to fix them.

A disquieting question begged for an answer: "Are students learning anything?" Could they write better, think better, work better, and understand the world better because of my teaching? I had to admit the evidence was mixed. When I looked at their papers and exams, I was often appalled. Term papers regularly disappointed me. Of course, there was always the shining exception—a brilliant essay, a surprising question, a penetrating comment. Those offered hope.

But the intellectual murk, illiteracy actually, that lurked beneath superficial exchanges daunted me. I first thought it was *me*. Maybe I was a phony, as I scrambled every day and into the night to read, think, and keep just ahead of the syllabus in the hope of justifying my academic robes. Then I began to think it was them, the students who didn't read and didn't think and didn't seem to care. Mostly I labored on and ignored these feelings.

I was lecturing one cold Tuesday morning in February—the pits of the academic year. My lecture concerned the political ideas of Immanuel Kant, one of those philosophers quoted frequently, but seldom read because of his doggedly difficult texts. I was explaining Kant's idea of the categorical imperative. It's a rule that he thought could be applied in any situation and result in a morally correct decision. I had read and lectured on this topic for 6 years. After struggles, on that fatal day I nailed it. I was brilliant in my exposition and phrases. The moment was so sweet that I stepped back to admire myself and look for the students' admiration. What I saw ripped my joy like a chainsaw. Some students were sleeping, some were reading newspapers, some were leaving the room, and worse, a third of them weren't there.

I lost it. "You," I commanded a scribbling student in the first row, "What are you writing?" "I'm taking notes, professor," she answered.

"And what did you just write?" She grabbed her notebook and held it up defensively. "I wrote that Kant said we can't tell lies because that's against the categories . . . or something. You were talking so fast . . ." I grasped the lectern hard and took a breath. "No, no, that's not it. That's not what I said."

"Yes it was. You said Kant wrote that even if a murderer asked, you had to obey the categoric thing."

"That's his conclusion, yes; but the important thing is the argument. I just outlined the argument. It shows how the categorical imperative works in practice . . ." Books closed, pens clicked, back packs zipped, and students tuned out as the period ended. I reached for a shred of authority and announced, "Class dismissed."

Something changed on that day. It wasn't as if I lost my innocence or became disillusioned. I knew from my student days that lectures weren't the best way to foster learning. But I thought I could make them provocative and inspiring. Maybe I was teaching as well as I could, but they weren't learning. Maybe I was a failure. Failures are scary but they can also make you curious. Four-wheel-drive doubt can take you far into the unknown.

I started with what felt like a bold move. I asked for volunteers to let me read their notes. I collected three or four sets of notes at the end of each class. Reading them was an eye-opening experience. I saw little or no resemblance between what I said and what they wrote. Questions were recorded as declarations; statements as questions; major points were missing, asides ended up listed as headings. What in the world was going on? Some students did learn, but it was clear that most of them did not get it.

It took me a while to figure out what they were doing. Finally, I saw their stumbling errors, and awkward reasoning, the ad hoc leaps of logic, and the distortions simply meant they were guessing. I tried stopping in the middle of my lectures, walked around the room, and asked questions: "What did that mean to you?" "What did you think of that?" "Did the chart confuse you?" "Do you disagree?" Brave students would sometimes start a discussion and I'd try to bring in others. But too often the students shut down like a covey of hunted quails. I tried an old trick. "Let's take a break," and let the students stand, stretch, and move around while I left the room. When I heard a discussion start, I would sidle back into a conversation about the day's topics. That helped some, but the more I read their notes, interviewed them, and answered their questions, the more complex the learning process looked.

I also started really listening to students and when I did I could hear my sorrows in their vacillation between understanding and getting by. Determined to face the problems, I fell more and more into conversations, listening and responding. Was talking less the only way to improve lectures?

Why Lectures Can't Be Fixed

Benjamin Bloom's (1953) early study of student thinking in lectures found that students face a paradox; (a) pay attention to what the lecturer says, or (b) find a way to connect that information to their own experiences. They need to make the lecture material meaningful by recalling related information, maybe finding examples, creating hypothetical applications, or generating questions. If the student does (a) then there is no time to do (b) and vice versa. Students can become either recording devices or active thinkers; but not both. The seeming chaos of discussion promotes confronting failures, thinking through applications, and conjuring alternatives, all of which aid in learning.

Routinely, lectures promote memorizing. That requires everything to be reduced to information as if lists of concepts, ideas, dates, problem types, formulas, and principles constituted human knowledge. Consequently, students barely remember the material for more than a few weeks and they can rarely transfer what they remember to new situations or problems. And most lectures are boring. Page Smith (1990) discovered students in his Dante seminar thought that the worst hell they could devise for professors who neglected students was to condemn them to listen to lectures for all eternity.

"I have never been able to feel the same way about lecturing since," he wrote (p. 214).

Students spend hours a day seated, quiet, and listening. Collegiate classrooms are scenes of stimulus deprivation, I suppose to make professors more intriguing. Classrooms are painted dull colors and the chairs are devilishly uncomfortable. Staring at the backs of heads is an opiate. Watching the learned professor talk, declaim, and even mumble seldom matches even the allure of daytime television. So the mystery remains—lectures fail to capture students' attention and they fail to fill minds with important information, but they still prevail. And I think maybe I know the reason.

Most professors have learned a lot despite having been subjected to many lectures. If professors figured out how, then students should be able to figure it out. If they can, then they're special and can find a home in their professor's field. How do professors learn from lectures? Most of them don't like to remember all the mistakes, the frustration and turmoil that were part of it. They remember the long hours that proved their intellectual muster. What professors did, they believe, students should do. But students are not like professors. Many of them get by in their courses, they forget what they may have learned, and then they go on to learn in their lives.

Often, we respond to the failure of lectures by trying to patch them up. Programs and centers that conduct courses on how to improve lectures are common. Googling the question turns up 49 million items. The advice you find is terrific—tell a story, organize around the most important ideas, raise questions, be dramatic, provide outlines or starter notes, train students to take notes, refer questions back to student groups for discussion, pose problems, provide cartoons and graphics, present cases, use lots of examples and analogies, and so on. All of these activities make lectures more palatable for professors and students but there is only spotty evidence that they improve learning. Closely examined, these practices are antilecture; they imply that the less instructors lecture the better they may teach. Improve-the-lecture practices are handcuffed to failure. They are kludges that work around inherent failures.

Merely jazzing up lectures with nonlecture activities will have limited impact on student learning. Instead, we need to explore our ignorance by expanding the repertoire of teaching. We can't be satisfied with what works (poorly) but need to strategically fail, to discover more effective classroom activities. That I think is the story of my experience with lectures.

I ended up with a new vision for teaching—an intricate game of give and take, conjecture and refutation, enthusiasm and criticism where all could fail and learn. To make it work required designed maps of the domain to be learned. The drive to cover material—transfer information—runs counter to the need for design. Iteration is key to both the student and the instructor roles; again and again to try, to fail, to recover, and improve. It was an approach far removed from lecturing.

It isn't enough to know that lectures fail. We have to know why they do and why they persist in spite of that. In an age of information technology when presentation of "anytime anywhere" information is possible, it is a waste of faculty talent to be lecturing. Student-directed reading wins hands down in any contest of retention and transfer. It's time to put lectures on the shelf.

References

Arons, A. B. (1997). *Teaching introductory physics.* Wiley.

Bligh, D. A. (2000). *What's the use of lectures?* Jossey-Bass.

Bloom, B. (1953). Thought processes in lectures and discussion. *Journal of General Education, 7*(3), 160–169.

Mazur, A. (2009, January). Farewell, lecture? *Science, 323*(2), 50–51.

McKeachie, W. J. (1986). *Teaching tips: A guidebook for the beginning college teacher* (8th ed.). Heath and Company.

Romer, A. S. (1971). *The vertebrate body.* Saunders.

Smith, P. (1990). *Killing the spirit: Higher education in America.* Viking Penguin.

Weiman, C. (2017). *Improving how universities teach science: Lessons from the Science Education Initiative.* Harvard University Press.

4

WHAT'S THE ROLE OF QUESTIONS IN LEARNING?

To improve what was happening in classrooms, Seymour Sarason (2002) suggested we make students' questions central. But don't teacher questions promote student thought and questions? The answer is no, if questions are being used as disciplinary devices, to find out who's done the reading. The answer is no, if the person asking the questions is the brightest and most active person in the room and the one who's using questions as a way to perform. It's long been assumed that the teacher's prodding encourages students to ask their own questions. The problem is that it doesn't work. Teacher questions dominate. Student questions languish. What happens in most classrooms trains students *not* to ask questions. My goal in this chapter is to elaborate on these points.

Based on observations in classrooms from kindergarten through college, Sarason came to these conclusions about questions: (a) students ask few questions, (b) instructors ask many questions that students must answer, (c) students can't admit they don't know without seeming to be stupid, (d) instructors only rarely discuss learning or teaching failures with colleagues or administrators, and (e) instructors are pressured to cover ever more content in less time in increasingly large courses. For him the first two observations were the most significant. Most of the time in most classes, teachers ask questions, students don't.

Remarkably, researchers who observe in classrooms have been documenting and criticizing the same pattern since the middle of the 19th century. Teachers ask a question, students offer short answers, teachers ignore those answers, and move to ask another question. As early as 1860, Thomas Morrison complained that beginning teachers confused rapid questioning with effective teaching. Fifty years later Romiett Stevens (1912) did 4 years' worth of observations in 100 New York City classes taught by highly regarded teachers. Most questions probed to see if the students could remember what they had heard or read. On average, teachers asked two to three questions per minute. Stevens saw that questioning teachers worked hard, more like "drillmasters" than "educators." These were not classrooms where students displayed their knowledge or ones that provided them the opportunities they needed to become self-reliant, independent thinkers.

More recently, teachers have used questioning to reduce lecturing. Asking students questions promised to involve students more actively and at the same time helped teachers manage the growing enrollments. Lectures bore students, and when bored, students are prone to mischief. So questioning can also be a successful strategy for controlling students at the same time it furthers teacher authority. Questioning has become the standard way to conduct discussions. It's considered an essential part of teaching and much literature advises teachers on ways to improve questioning so that students' answers and questions will also improve.

Making Questions Central

In the same sense Sarason suggested making questions central, I thought I could light student fires with my questions. Since students must think to learn, and since questions promoted thought, I reasoned that my questions would promote learning, especially if I used the Socratic method. I was impressed by the claims that aggressive questions promoted better learning,

I handed out study questions in an introductory political science course and told the class that I would be using the Socratic method and planned to call on them randomly. When I did, they would stand and answer my questions until excused. That would give everyone the chance to think on their feet. It would motivate them to prepare for class which, of course, would aid in their understanding of Plato.

To ensure success, I decided I would call on the best female student in the class first. That would challenge the males.

"Julia," she rose to her feet. "How does Kant define enlightenment?" I asked firmly. She started to speak, and then looked down at her clenched fingers.

"Oh come on," I coaxed, "You know. Now, just relax."

A long ugly silence followed. I couldn't believe it, she was fighting tears and wouldn't look at me. I repeated my explanation of how Socratic questioning improved student learning skills. Pretty soon no one in the class would look at me.

Professors are not supposed to fail. They know the texts, the questions, the answers, and the pedagogy. Failures mean you aren't qualified; you can't profess. When you do flop you feel a shiver—as if you stood on a windy road with your pants down. I felt that shiver, saw ugliness ahead in the course, and panicked. "Please sit down," I croaked.

She sat staring at her textbook. Pacing, I looked at the ceiling, banged into a desk, and announced the end of Socratic questioning. Relief spread like the end of a long-held breath. "That wasn't such a good idea," I confessed, desperate to get the class back on my side. "It seemed like a good idea when I read about it," I tried to shrug like James Dean. "Plato and Socrates used the method." Still there were no signs of forgiveness. "Now, let's just discuss the study questions I assigned."

Slowly a dialogue emerged. A student wearing a ball cap made a useful suggestion. "You know the study questions aren't such a bad idea. Could you hand them out every week?" I said yes and at the end of 50 minutes everything seemed normal—almost. I stopped Julia and apologized. She still wouldn't look at me. She dropped the course. No way around it, I had failed. There was something about the fundamentals of questioning that I had not learned.

How Babies Learn With Questions

If we assume that brain architecture determines how and what brains notice, questions are crucial. Infants start asking questions as soon as they can talk. "What's that?" "What's this?" "What if . . . ? "Is this like . . . ?" "What can it do?" "Can it do that . . . ?" "Where does it live?" "Why?" and "Why?" and "Why?" punctuates their conversations. Questions are their verbal tools for exploring the abstract world of concepts, causality, judgments, language, and other minds. Self-generated, their questions are relevant—that is, they request information that can improve their cognitive maps or representations of reality. Their questions provoke answers that produce novel expectations, correct erroneous assumptions, and bolster uncertain beliefs.

Researchers in child development have found that babies learn the world by testing their expectations through trial and error. Calling babies the best human learners (outside of scientists) Alison Gopnik et al. (1999) have put forward what they call the "theory theory" (p. 155). It states that children have theories about the world. They test their theories by applying them. When they don't get the result they expect, they learn by reformulating what they originally thought.

I interpret the theory this way: Babies learn by bootstrapping. They begin life with innate expectations of the world, the products of evolution. They expect their fundamental abstract structures to guide practice. That is their means of survival, but they have to work to do so. You might think of their minds as preformed with general categories, models, and theories about the world. Those built-in structures represent or map the world starting with simple charts that make exploration and experience of the world possible. As their first diagrams fail in practice, curiosity drives them to add or subtract features, or even try out new representations.

A philosopher of science, like Karl Popper (2014), would say infants begin with conjectures about what causes things to happen, what kinds of things there are in the world, or what gives pleasure and pain. As apprentice scientists, babies use their current theories to formulate new theories. The impetus is failure. When a theory doesn't work—expectations don't happen, categories don't discriminate, or results don't satisfy—they hypothesize new ones. Babies are terrific at that. In the laboratory when they fail to get desired results they easily come up with dozens of new hypotheses. They pull themselves up from their initial theories about the world by making more and more sophisticated models of reality. And they do this with astonishingly small numbers of observations; inferring causal links from a few instances. Said another way, they learn a lot from a few mistakes.

The process is similar for us. When our expectations fail, questions explode. You cannot learn from mistakes without questions. Was it a mistake? Did the theory fail? Was the diagnosis of the situation wrong? Was the observation relevant? Was the measurement accurate? All those questions are assumed in the what-went-wrong-and-how-do-I-correct-it question that we ask ourselves over and over when confronted with failed expectations.

Once again look at how infants deal with failed expectations. They grasp, throw, and suck, all deliberate investigations of the world organized by the brain's expectations. Objects fall, they don't rise, but they do—the balloon drifts to the ceiling, the bird flies for the high branch, how did that happen? Objects are stable; but they are not—momma's face disappears behind the pillow, it is gone and then it delightfully reappears; did it go somewhere? Watch a red ball fall and get smaller as it bounces down the stairs and then get bigger as brother fetches it back; was that the same ball? Knock a spoon on the floor, mother picks up, knock again mother gets vexed, knock again, mother takes away the Cheerios; is that how mothers are—they help and then they get mad? The child's world may be complex and surprising, but it isn't chaotic.

Research in the neurosciences affirms that brains select crucial instances in experience; they don't wait for the world to type in data. Brains seek relevance to defend themselves from overwhelming stimuli and the tyranny of things. Never passive, brains choose, match, and build ever more exacting models of reality. Using generalized patterns as guides, they select from the mélange of life. By the time a brain reaches college it has formed unique and complex representations, narratives, if you will, or maps, with which the brain scans the world for a few important things and ignores pretty much everything else. A professor trying to gain the attention of an undergraduate brain is like shouting a joke at a roaring party and hoping to be heard. To teach we must create situations that grab, perplex, and yet support students. I lay out how to do this in several of the chapters to come.

Authentic questions can also highlight differences and connections, as well as conflicts. Queries can tell us whether we make sense to others, or if not; and whether we understand them, or if we don't. Questions can shock or beguile us from our complacent views of reality. Social encounters reward us with novel questions that show minds at work on different sides of a topic. The resulting conflicts incite the critical reasoning described in chapter 9. They can turn differences into deliberations. The easiest ways outside our mental boxes are encounters with those who don't see the world as we do. Once outside, we're in a place where we can reflect on what we know and how well we know it. At their most profound, questions reveal our ignorance in a changing complex world. That can fuel innovations. No wonder then that we expect questions to be important in the classroom. And no wonder that students are held back when they can't ask them.

How Do Questions Function in Teaching?

How do you enter the mind of a student? For a teacher to work effectively she must understand the experience of learning what she is teaching. But that perspective is illusive, if not impossible. Once we know something as experts, it is nearly impossible for us to imagine a mind without that knowledge. Psychologists have found that it even affects 4-year-olds, who when they know that a cookie is in a box, cannot conceive that others do not know that.

Instructors cannot directly comprehend the mental representations of their students. Brains are too unique and experience too specific. Even better, students themselves need to know if their understandings and assumptions about the world are reliable. That motivates and directs their curiosity. Students who have an idea of what they don't know and want to know are prepared to learn. Their questions signal thought, give clues as to their mental representations, and can be what teachers need to supply relevant contexts and exercises.

To see learning in the college classroom is to hear students' questions. Teaching without them is an anxious and rapid display of knowledge and ideals. What the teacher needs to know is whether students are reconstructing their models of the world. Just as an author must consider the reader's situation, and the speaker consider the audience's attitudes, an instructor must guess what students are thinking. Teachers can probe student thinking with questions. But based on being interrogated by teachers in previous courses, students have come to believe that when teachers ask questions, they want particular answers. So students try to tell teachers what they want to hear. They protect their misunderstandings and don't ask what they really want to know.

In the classroom, we want students to consider and evaluate their mental structures—to reflect on how and what they know. That makes their questions precious. Without them, teaching is more difficult and learning becomes private. We know from experience and research that students' questions reveal what they know, what blocks their understanding, and what interests them. Without such insights we teach blindly, dependent on happy accidents. We offer an example that sparks interests or tell a story that taps secret curiosities. We know that student questions like "Could we apply that to . . . ?," "Is this like . . . ?," "Doesn't that contradict . . . ?," or "What will happen if . . . ?" indicate learning in progress. Student questions guide teachers; they are what direct student learning.

Maybe Teachers Could Ask Better Questions

James Dillon was an award-winning conventional high school teacher noted for high standards, harsh discipline, and tough grading. After 5 years of what he characterized as pleasant but fruitless classes, he was exasperated. Teaching and learning remained mysteries. He knew how to get students to work but not how to get them to learn. To get students more involved in learning, he experimented with grades, tests, and compulsory attendance. He got rid of tests, graded assignments, and made attendance optional. In class, students were free to talk about or question anything.

His radical violation of classroom policies and practice disturbed everyone and some of his innovations were mistakes, but some of his unconventional methods worked. His colleagues started recognizing that students became skilled learners in his courses. Dillon's various experiments convinced him that education should consist of what students want and need.

A meticulous and persistent scholar, Dillon (2004), thought educators got questions wrong. His research found that classroom discussions were dominated by teacher questions, a student response, and another teacher question. Most teachers weren't aware of how many and how often they asked questions, how little time they allowed for answers, and how they ignored the answers given. Moreover, they asked too many questions that could be answered yes, no, or with a couple of words—questions that relied on the ability to recall what the teacher said or what appeared in the text.

The analysis of teacher questioning methods has led some reformers to recommend that instructors ask intellectually provocative questions, wait longer for students to respond, and pay more attention to their answers. They operated on the assumption that more sophisticated teacher questions would prompt more profound student questions. When those reforms were evaluated the results showed exactly the opposite occurred. More and better teacher questions led to fewer student questions. Decades of exhortations, workshops, and manuals have done nothing to reduce the high ratio of teacher to student questions. Attempts to ask better questions encouraged teachers to keep asking questions. Dillon finally concluded that encouraging teacher questions of any sort suppressed student questions. It's the questions students ask that feed curiosity, not the didactic ones asked by their teachers. When students seek answers to the questions they ask, that kick-starts learning.

Dillon wondered if other professions made better use of questions and so he surveyed therapists, crime investigators, and job interviewers. He found that professionals who want to know what people think and believe don't interrogate. Their techniques involve prompts that encourage candid reflection and the elaboration of thoughts, emotions, and recollections. Questions, these professionals told him, trigger defenses and shut down responses. They rely on other techniques such as silence, encouragement, invitations, and declarative statements. Professionals in the social sciences and litigating attorneys use questions to squeeze responses into short usable answers. They ask only questions to which they know the most likely answers.

How these contrasting professional groups get information from respondents confirmed what Dillon had concluded about questions in classrooms. Teacher questions get limited answers, but avoiding questions stimulates more expansive thoughts and information. For example, declarations about matters at hand promote questions and pushback. If I state my opinions, you will likely state yours and maybe criticize mine. A question requests a piece of information—that's it. And when it's answered, digressions and further thought no longer appear necessary. Make a declaration and it leads to thought, arguments, and deliberation.

In the standard question situation, it's assumed the questioner does not know the answer but someone else does; the questioner needs the answer; the information required is specified; the questioner believes the presuppositions of the question are true; and the questioner expects at least one true answer. Educators violate all of these assumptions. The teacher/questioner knows the answer, doesn't need the answer, won't specify the required information, makes erroneous presuppositions about the nature of questions, and expects incorrect answers. When students ask questions, in contrast, they don't know the answer, need the answer, can specify the information needed, presuppose that questions can resolve quandaries, and expect a useful answer.

Teaching with questions is futile because the practice is infallible. There are no possibilities of failure and thus no opportunities to improve. It works like astrology. The teacher probes for preconceived answers. If successful, the student announces the right answer and that is called learning. If the student can't reproduce the right answer, then that is a failure to learn. I write here from my own experience. I questioned students for years. I thought I was doing good. It was the right way to teach. But I always wished the technique worked better than it did. I should have spent more time wondering why it didn't.

What Happens When Students Start Asking Questions?

It was a class on Karl Marx's philosophy and the topic was alienation—the notion that people can be dehumanized in a system where they and their work is bought and sold. The student was a cheerleader, trained to be strong, agile, and attractive. Spending hours in practice and travel, cheerleaders are overworked and often perfectionists. She enacted a perfect "see I'm listening" student in class. And then she asked this question: "Why is it that if I sell my body to someone, that's awful and illegal; but if someone (and she paused to look at me) sells their brain, that's okay?"

The room exploded. "Your body isn't a thing, it's you." "Aren't your ideas part of you?" "What about strength?" "Or looks?" "We all have to live." "We have to sell something." "You can't sell babies." "Would you sell one of your kidneys if you were desperate?" "How about being a paid companion to someone dying?" "Don't artists sell their souls?" A cowboy riding herd on rampaging steers, I darted in and out, making sure everyone got to speak and that we kept moving through to cover the content. From the edge of the room I refereed. "You need evidence to back that up." "Wait, let him finish." "Let's stop and think about that." "Don't ignore her statement, either respond or wait." "Attacking Joe personally is outlawed."

After an hour, issues emerged. I framed them as questions and listed them on the board. The discussion wound down and the students settled into the routine of "go ahead and tell us what all this means." And I took the bait and fell back into my role as faculty explainer. The period ended, satchel on my shoulder, tired but satisfied, I followed them out the door.

But I wasn't happy. The students had encountered their ignorance. They were of the consensus that markets on the whole were a good thing. But they had entered a snarly area where buying and selling conflicted with moral sentiment. As human institutions, markets were, of course, imperfect; they could and did fail. These juniors and seniors would soon be on the labor market. Most still didn't know who they were or what they wanted to do, but already they were writing advertisements for themselves. They were in a sense alienated, shaping and selling themselves to please others; to earn a living, and to be good children. Education made them marketable, but unknown forces determined their value. And although adults told them they should follow their dreams, job interviews darkened their futures.

Mark St. John (1999) describes this pedagogical failure. He suggests that we think of our knowledge of the world as a bubble. Inside we are comfortable with what we see and experience. New information is assimilated to fit the filing cabinets of our knowledge. If it doesn't fit, we ignore or deny it. Outside that bubble lies our ignorance; what we don't know and even don't know we don't know. If we push against our limits we move into the zone of proximal ignorance. There we can entertain alternatives and perhaps improve our representations. That improvement St. John calls *learning*. The movement from bubble to ignorance he calls *inquiry*.

Too often in the classroom instructors assign problems and help students come up with possible solutions. Those solutions are night patrols to probe the no man's land of ignorance. But the curriculum intervenes, and instructors halt the process. "That's it, we've come up with a solution, now let's get on with the next topic." My students ventured into their zone of proximal ignorance. And in my wisdom, I said "good job" and moved on. St. John points out that here is what we want students to get good at—finding the limits of how they see the world. We want them to recognize that they don't know something that is important to them, become fascinated with their particular ignorance, and take a first step beyond what they already know. As St. John (1999) writes, "A learner has to become a connoisseur of their ignorance" (p. 9).

All the practices basic to learning—seeking, trying, failing, recovering, discussing, innovating, pushing on to the zone of proximal ignorance—are not possible without students who ask questions. Yet it still goes against classroom norms for students to display ignorance, perplexity, or the need to know. It goes against educational culture for teachers to admit their ignorance or perplexity. It goes against the expert status of professors to admit they practice in a sea of ignorance. In education we cannot promote student questions unless we insist on the freedom to question our own practices and assumptions.

That was Sarason's insight. Those of us who consider ourselves educators need questions that shatter certainty. Do lectures waste time? Does grading papers improve learning? Are students gaining knowledge or accumulating information? What if each student learns differently? How can I get the time to design learning experiences? Where can I find more flexible spaces? How do I find out what the students are thinking? Can I better use student energies and passion? Am I effective? Do I have enough time? Must I cling to the tools that make classrooms manageable? Dare I challenge students, administrators, alumni, and the public? Can I admit that I don't know the answers?

Rarely do these kinds of authentic questions get asked. Given that, professors, teachers, and students must be foolhardy to ask them. That goes double for the concerned reformers who try to drag our educational system into the 21st century. Reform too requires that we learn from failure. When we start asking the questions we can't answer, we jumpstart learning.

And One Final Thought

The question "Why do schools suppress student questions?" is a Socratic question of the best sort. It is real because we don't know the answer. We can only speculate. It is promising in the sense that any answers to it will promote more questions, opening new fields of inquiry. And it reveals ignorance about practices we thought were settled and known. I love the question! It's a perfect example of the absolutely essential role questions play in learning. When I finally asked the question, my attempts to answer it revealed a promising ignorance. It kicked me out of my knowledge bubble and made my mistakes intriguing.

I wanted to write a book that asked ask real questions and explored possible answers. I am not concerned that you agree with my answers or ideas, but I fervently hope the questions I'm raising will lead you to questions about habitual teaching practices and the resulting failure of students to learn. Dillon described my predicament in writing a book like this. All reformers are teachers. They want people to change their views. They want them to learn. But how do you get ideas across when you don't believe that teaching is a matter of getting ideas across? How do you get people to change their view when only they can build a new view? When I am most determined to tell you, I am most inclined to ignore what you know, and that would be fatal to my enterprise.

References

Dillon, J. T. (2004). *Questioning and teaching: A manual of practice.* Resource Publications.

Gopnik, A., Meltzoff, A. N., & Kuhl, P. K. (1999). *The scientist in the crib: Minds, brains, and how children learn.* William Morrow & Co.

Popper, K. (2014). *Conjectures and refutations: The growth of scientific knowledge.* Routledge.

Sarason, S. (2002). *Educational reform: A self-scrutinizing memoir.* Teachers College Press.

Stevens, R. (1912). *The question as a measure of instructional efficiency: A critical study of classroom practice.* Teachers College, Columbia University.

St. John, M. (1999). *Wait don't tell me!* Workshop Center. https://inverness-research.org/reports/1999-09-Rpt-waitdonttellme-polinqlc.PDF

5

CONTENT

Does All That Information Lead to Knowledge?

It's not just lectures and teacher questions that are a problem when it comes to learning. We've got courses crammed with ever-increasing amounts of content. Curriculum design focuses, not on activities that help student learning, but on how to manage mountains of information in the course. We no longer understand the differences between knowledge and information. The relationship between the two is complex, but the point I want to make in this chapter is straightforward. The accumulation of information does not automatically lead to knowledge. More content in a course does not automatically mean more learning in the course. Why that's true makes sense if we understand what knowledge is, how it relates to information, and most importantly, how we help students develop theirs. But first we need to start with this age of information and how it made us prize information over knowledge.

Information Everywhere

We're drowning in information. That's the threat, the news, and the cliché. So accessible, cheap, and automatic, this information overwhelms us. It sprays from our cellphones, floods our inboxes, and swamps our scholarship. But the problem is not new. Historian Ann Blair (2010) has pointed out that even in the ancient and medieval worlds scholars complained about too many books, not enough time, and the difficulty of remembering all that was known.

Today hoarding information is at the heart of what universities do. Accumulating it requires a host of tools from alphabetized indexes, tables, catalogues, and bibliographies to dissertations, textbooks, encyclopedias, and data bases. Digital technology has opened the floodgates of information. Downstream academic institutions receive and contribute more to the deluge. Large buildings, libraries, laboratories, computer centers, and air-conditioned servers support postsecondary education's role in the creation and preservation of information. But all this brings more laments than celebrations.

New information technologies make life more hectic and confusing. It is not just the technology, buildings, and people required to manage all information, but the toll on human well-being, time, and productivity also add to the chaos. Work interruptions, long searches, 24-hour message assaults, and email from everywhere all seem to lower human creativity and satisfaction. Traditionally, information was a treasure to be bottled and protected. Now it seems more effluent; to be contained, treated, and expelled.

Most obstreperously the internet is awash in information and Russell Ackoff (1988) equates information with descriptions that answer basic questions such as who, what, when, and where. Google "information" and receive nearly 9 billion items in .40 seconds. Although this information is portable and easily transferred, it is also transient. The fact that the temperature in Madrid is 40 degrees is not very useful unless we know whether it's Madrid, Spain or Madrid, Maine; whether it's Fahrenheit or Celsius; the season, the time of day, and what the temperature will be tomorrow when we plan to visit.

Being inundated with information from the media, the internet, and social networks makes it harder to figure out what we want or need to know. The volume, velocity, and shapelessness of the information makes it all but useless. When we try to drink, we drown. We can't handle the quantity, suspect the quality, and feel guilty about not keeping up. We don't know as much as we should and that makes us vulnerable to fraud and deception (Wurman, 2001).

Feeling anxious, we find it more difficult to make judgments confidently and are less likely to pursue what interests us. Wurman (2001) thinks one cause of this is the way we are taught how to learn, namely the importance placed "on puzzle solving and memorization" (p. 238). The accumulate-preserve-produce-transmit focus of higher education exacerbates the condition. Rather than trying to gulp down this information ocean, students (in fact, all of us) would do better if we learned to navigate it. We need to find out what we need to know and ignore the rest. That requires knowledge, not undigested information.

As information has become plentiful and cheap, knowledge seems to be rarer and more expensive. To be useful, information must be compiled, updated, corrected, protected, and accessed. It used to be hard to collect, protect, and copy frail manuscripts. To find the best information, scholars had to travel and qualify for entry into a library or university. The tasks of maintenance and transmission were so time-consuming that the information was easily confused with knowledge.

These conditions, writes David Cohen, constitute our instructional inheritance, a major source of the persistence of traditional teaching practice (Cohen, 1988). In the Middle Ages, European educators worked from hand-copied manuscripts and fragments salvaged from the disintegration of the Roman Empire. The texts were rare and often sacred. As Cohen notes, they were read, studied, and analyzed with close attention and reverence. Scholars took pride in memorizing and expounding on them. Reverence for the text bolstered belief in the authority and objectivity of information. During the Reformation, Protestants sought out and publicized textual sources that the Church had long monopolized. This added to the popular veneration of written words. Cohen argues that the respect for the authority of the written text endures.

Scientists replaced the sanctity of revealed text with the authority of objective, rational, and natural facts supposedly based on systematic observation and measurement. Over time the conjectures of science were treated as doctrines. Thus, books with their facts retained their authority and demanded new devotion. Still worse, the representations of knowledge on the printed page were treated as information; purpose and action were stripped away leaving teachers and students to deal primarily with learning *that* not *how*. The internet seems to have completely erased the old distinction between knowledge and information.

In the absence of true knowledge, undigested information often takes on the veneer of "truth." Some of those who cruise the Web treat all facts, opinions, wisdom, and rants as more or less equal, provided that they conform to their preconceived notions. Put another way, knowledge tends to be drowned out by information. In courses, it's information that's transferred to students, and the reputation of the course and its instructor hinge on how much information the course contains. We never question how much information is enough. The assumption stands: More is always better.

Content: Quantity Trumps Quality

Once we confuse knowledge with information then, "content" derails course design. "Content" traps us in the old conduit metaphors of teaching—the more that gets pushed through the pipe the better. The teacher's goal is an ever-increasing efficiency in transmitting that information. If students are lucky, the information might be useful someday. Since we can't predict that—both the relevance and accuracy of information change rapidly—there's pressure to add still more materials, just in case the student needs to know it. Content is contained in the professor's head, the course's textbooks, slides or charts, and library resources. It must be transferred from these containers into the minds of the students. But minds are not containers. That is the metaphor-busting news of the cognitive revolution that I'm dealing with in the upcoming chapter on learning.

This mode of talking and thinking about content and coverage makes some sense if we recognize how much textbooks determine course designs. Consider the growing size (and cost) of textbooks that are revised to include more and more topics and information. Bigger books require pictures and textual gimmicks to keep students awake and reading what for them are dull, dense narratives. And still, there's this sense that we can't get all of the content into the textbooks, cover all of it in the course, or transmit enough of it in the curriculum. How can we expect that course designs dictated by what needs to be covered will be anything but jumbled and bloated?

When the iPod was a new device, I used it in workshops, first pointing out it's slim, sleek, and elegant design. To achieve that design its authors selected the most important user features and cut or hid the rest. Then I'd show a TV remote control. Complex and clumsy, the large (some are small) slab of plastic I showed was covered with a myriad of buttons. Large or small, most remotes are still hard to use. Their design puts priority on adding features while it ignores the user's needs. Then I'd ask participants to consider the typical course design. Is it more like an iPod or a TV remote?

I've tried to use that analogy to guide professors' course designs and they laugh—nervously. "So begin," I say "by thinking about two or three central ideas in your course that you want your students to be able to use right now." But there are more than that, comes the reply. I counter by saying that to learn an important idea and its uses takes time. Students have to deliberately practice, which means they must attempt to apply their learning, make errors, and recover from them. If you throw a large number of ideas at the students, they will either learn a select few based on their interests or they won't learn any. If teachers want to design courses that promote learning, then they must limit the number of topics just as the design team at Apple had to choose limited functions.

I once went through that routine with a bright, newly hired faculty member. He needed to redesign several traditional courses as problem-based offerings. "But if we take all that time in class to work through problems, how will I cover the content?" he objected.

"What content?" I snapped, "Let's talk about what you want your students to be able to do at the end of the course. What is it you want them to learn?" I continued to prod him to pare down the topics that could be practiced and learned in 15 weeks. At the end of what was supposed to be our first consultation, he looked at me and winked. "I get it," he said, "just the big ideas." I left pleased and headed home for a bone-chilling martini. The next day the dean called: "Could you stop by for a chat?" Once in the administrative sanctum I learned the truth. The faculty member blew the whistle: "He wants me to dumb down the course," he told my boss.

So what went wrong? How did content quantity, the amount of information, become so much more important than knowledge? I'm trying to make the case that the so-called "information revolution" has had the perverse effect of causing us to fill our courses with information which leaves us to hope students will figure out what to do with all they're being taught. I think we need a "knowledge revolution" with the potential to make students (and the rest of us) better thinkers and knowledge persons. But that kind of revolution will only happen if we understand why collecting information doesn't lead to knowledge, insight, or anything close to wisdom.

The Differences Between Information and Knowledge

Usually we lump data, facts, observations, generalizations, theories, and judgments into a category we call either knowledge, information, or data. Many authors have tried to differentiate between them. Ackoff, for example, made these distinctions: *data* represent properties of observed objects, images, quantities and magnitudes; example: "there are seven trees in the yard"; *information* is descriptions inferred from data; "my backyard is shady"; and *knowledge* is know-how—the production of desired outcomes; example: "To grow a productive garden I must cut down some trees." Here is another way to express the distinction: Knowledge consists of patterns and information consists of descriptions (Meehan, 1988, p. 2). The patterns are "organized human experience" with "organized" being key term. Data is what we select from the booming, flashing world we sense. Information is what we select from data. Knowledge consists of selected information organized into useful models.

This seems abstract if not abstruse, but it's really not that difficult. Let's imagine you're headed to the beach for a week. You need information about locations, distances, places to stay, costs, crowds, beach conditions, and other amenities. To actually experience a vacation, you need knowledge to guide your choice of where you are going, how to get there, what to take, and what to do when you get there. In short you need to decide and plan. Knowledge is not mysterious, it is just a model, in this case, of a vacation. It organizes information, guides your search and selection of data, and enables you to get in a loaded car and head for the Outer Banks.

Scientific knowledge is much more complex and precise, of course, but your vacation plan and Rutherford's model of the atom are both human representations of reality. Note that the information without the plan is useless and collecting it would be endless. You can have lots of information, but without knowledge chances are good you'll make poor decisions. Also note that without the information, the plan would be at best "uninformed." If Google maps offers you two routes to the Outer Banks, but you don't understand the difference between getting there by freeway or backroads, you've got one chance out of two to make a bad choice. To enjoy and act in the world requires the integration of both information and knowledge.

Similarly, authors distinguish between two kinds of learning: "learning about" or receiving transmitted skills and information; and "learning to be" or applying knowledge in specific contexts. (Thomas & Brown, 2009). Indeed, most educators assume that there is a difference between "the basics" that need to be memorized and "higher order knowledge" that must be learned through more demanding deliberate practice, application, and analysis. The ringers here are "basic" and "higher order" and the damaging assumptions about accumulation and transcendence that they entail. The empiricist dogma has it that piles of data ("big data" as it is called today) can result in carefully sorted mountains of information that somehow reach up and become higher knowledge.

Data, information, and knowledge are complimentary, but they aren't progressive summaries or independent categories. Data and information don't come first and knowledge later. As learners we start with representations that are sharpened and refined over time. Based on those understandings, our representations of reality; we anticipate, predict, and make choices. These distinctions are important. Our thinking about them is hampered when they are lumped together in an undifferentiated way. Information and knowledge are distinct but still connected. Their relationship is complex and understanding it begins with knowing what knowledge is and how it develops.

A Deeper Understanding of Knowledge

It was Gilbert Ryle (1945) who distinguished *knowing how* from *knowing that,* but he also insisted the two are complimentary. We learn how through deliberate practice and what we learn from this error-focused practice inextricably links knowledge to action. Dougald Hine suggests this example. Take a bus timetable. Here is information organized in patterns of times, places, and sequences. If all we do is carry it around or memorize it, the timetable is only information. If, on the other hand, we integrate use of the timetable into our existing knowledge of a particular part of the city, it can guide our movements to work, shopping, restaurants, and friends. The schedule becomes a useful knowledge component that enables us to cope successfully with our environment. Hine notes that the difference between information and knowledge is "the difference between memorizing the bus timetable for a city you will never visit and using that timetable to explore a city in which you have just arrived" (Hine, 2014).

Knowledge then can be used to control our environment. Patterns are conjectured and constructed with past information or descriptions of things and relations among them. Forecasts, theories, and policies allow us to anticipate what is likely to happen, to make something happen, or to decide what we want to happen. Knowledge originates and is first applied inside our minds. It allows us to analyze, plan, and critique before we act. Since knowledge can exist only in someone's head, it can't be transferred in the way that information and data can.

Knowledge isn't observed, it is created by inferring, guessing, combining, questioning, generalizing, applying, and testing. Knowledge takes collected information and creates patterns such as models, maps, schemas, or theories. Without such patterns, information is of minimal use. But without information the reliability of the patterns is unknown. Knowledge then is know-how—using our unique representations built on information to control results.

To guide the actions we take, we need patterns that hold over time and space. General patterns must hold for the vast majority of times and places including those yet to come. If I know that A causes B today, I can perform A in the future and achieve B, at least most of the time. Our patterns, or understandings, enable us to make decisions because they ignore irrelevant details and they work under most but not all conditions. You could say they are false, but more accurately they're approximations of reality. The jury is always out on their reliability. Knowledge requires criticism. Use is the test of knowledge—try it out, does it solve the problem or answer the question? A lot of times it does not, but failure provides the opportunity to acquire more information, develop a new understanding, and then that knowledge can be tested. Chapter 8 explains more about why and how mistakes and failure are essential to learning.

Economists are fond of reducing knowledge to information to make it a commodity that can be treated as property and analyzed in terms of markets.

Indeed, it is all too easy to fall into the empiricist trap of assuming that more information makes knowledge more reliable. The fallacy is to believe we can improve a map by adding more and more details until we have created an exact copy of the terrain itself. The alternative is to be aware of the importance of applying knowledge to expose its limits and weaknesses.

You can't just memorize models and maps. You have to understand them and their limitations so that you can make the necessary corrections and adjustments to get the right results. The way you earn that ability to improvise is through many hours of application, that is, deliberate practice. A knowledge expert is not someone who knows tons of facts or can find them quickly on the phone. A knowledgeable expert is prepared like an athlete or musician to make spontaneous adjustments because she knows the limits of the models she uses. She can improve her representations when they fail.

Breakthroughs result when we examine and analyze those failures (Wurman, 2001, p. 244). Knowledge then requires deliberate practice and to teach knowledge requires the ability to design deliberate practice sessions. More coach than oracle, an expert teacher advances knowledge through intimate acquaintance with its weakness and powers. She needs to be a master of the ways in which knowledge can be organized, and the ways it can be learned. Plus, she must be able to closely observe student performances. An experimenter in design, practice, and evaluation, she collects careful data about learning results and analyzes it, which constitutes a form of experimentation. Learning demands understanding and recall of causes, effects, and connections. The patterns of knowledge—the maps, the schema, and the models—must be created by the individual learner. That is demanding work. But learning, although hard, is a joy when compared to the drudgery of memorizing answers to other people's questions.

All of this leads to yet another unavoidable conclusion about teaching in higher education. The expert teacher does not help students develop knowledge, expand and grow their understandings or representation of reality, by exposing them to mountains of information. Courses should not be content free, but they should contain only as much information as students need to confront their current understandings, to motivate them to raise questions about what they think they know, and provide opportunities for them to revise, expand, and otherwise improve their representations. Knowing *that* depends on information; knowing *how* requires knowledge.

References

Ackoff, R. L. (1989). From data to wisdom. *Journal of Applied Systems Analysis, 16*(3), 3–9.

Blair, A. M. (2010). *Too much to know: Managing scholarly information before the modern age.* Yale University Press.

Cohen, D. K. (1988). *Teaching practice: Plus ça change.* (ED299257). ERIC. https://files.eric.ed.gov/fulltext/ED299257.pdf

Hine, D. (2014, March 6). What good is information? *Aeon.* https://aeon.co/essays/how-can-we-be-bored-when-we-have-google

Meehan, E. J. (1988). *The thinking game: A guide to effective study.* Chatham House.

Ryle, G. (1945). Knowing how and knowing that. *The Aristotelian Society, 46*(1), 1–16.

Thomas, D., & Brown, J. S. (2009). Why virtual worlds can matter. *International Journal of Learning and Media, 1*(1), 37–49.

Wurman, R. S. (2001). *Information anxiety 2.* Que.

6

TEACHING REALITIES

Conflicts, Assumptions, and Approaches

At some point you are no longer a new teacher. My transition into that long midcareer section happened as cognitive science was revealing more and more about how brains learn. The revelations had mind-boggling implications for teaching, but what cognitive science is uncovering conflicts with long-standing assumptions and with the basic approaches to teaching.

Learning works in counter-intuitive ways, just as experience doesn't suggest that the round earth spins and tumbles through space. Likewise, we don't intuit that the brain creates the constant colors we see; encodes variations in light waves, sound waves, and air pressure into electrical signals and chemical transmitters to build representations of the world.

Since the neurosciences continually contradict our common sense, understanding learning requires us to doubt centuries of wisdom. We have been building universities and talking at students for more than a thousand years. This new brain knowledge primarily threatens those of us who most need to understand and use it. But consider this: We have learned more about how people learn in the past 60 years than in all of the rest of human history.

Educators are in a situation similar to 19-century medical practitioners when they were confronted by the idea that microbial infections caused disease. This new knowledge enabled doctors to treat and cure conditions that had long thwarted them. It also meant that their unintentional ignorance had infected and killed many patients. Wounded pride caused many physicians to reject and hound early pioneers in antiseptic techniques like Ignaz Semmelweis and Joseph Lister who advanced life-saving discoveries.

I experienced any number of confrontations as my own thinking about teaching changed while other teachers' thinking stayed the same. Thirty years into my career, in addition to teaching, I directed a program that supported professors with mentoring, assessment, and funding for innovations involving learning teams and knowledge applications in the classroom. Among many things I learned from directing this program, one of the most significant happened during a breakfast meeting with the administrator to whom I reported. Enthusiastic is a mild adjective for the claims of short-term successes I heard myself describing to him. He listened carefully, asked questions about budgets and staffing, and probed for failures. Proud and satisfied, I glowed like a plugged-in heater.

Slicing into his short stack of pancakes, my boss raised his eyes to give me a loan-shark look: "I worry that too much teaching will ruin your intellect." The comment pitched a chunk of omelet to the bottom of my stomach.

"But teaching is the most challenging thing I do," I sputtered. "It fascinates me, stretches my mind, and requires constant creativity. The need to find ways to connect students to knowledge keeps me busy reading and thinking. Every class is different. I always need to get better. Do you think I would work so hard at it if it were dull?"

He responded "What is challenging about telling students basic knowledge and testing them to make sure they learn it? Sure, it's part of your job to keep them interested. Doing a little of it can't hurt, but a full diet? That's boring. Research is what keeps your intellectual batteries charged."

I counterpunched. "Writing articles that no one reads, arguing with reviewers who reject new ideas, hassling with editors that crush prose into passive mush; you think that keeps my intellect churning?" Voice high, cheeks red, I continued: "Good teaching is research . . . "

His dark suit rising predicted a storm. His napkin hit the plate like a gauntlet and he shot out of the dining room. Subject closed. Before that breakfast I naively thought we understood each other. He had come to my presentations on quality improvements in the classroom. He had even attended my class and worked alongside students. He had led a campaign that generated funding for a center devoted to innovation in learning. And yet he didn't understand. His favorite word "change" meant something different than my ideas about "innovation." We never discussed the issue again. Outside a gusty November morning slapped my face.

Teaching Provokes Conflicts

The faculty I observed and worked with in the program I directed struggled with teaching and were perplexed by its demands. They worried about how to maintain the job slots that would keep their departments staffed well enough to get national attention. They sought to justify their standing as world-class scholars by publishing often and everywhere. They were skeptical of educational reforms, buzzwords, and fads. They saw themselves as embattled defenders of reason, rigor, and standards in a world swamped with information and cheap intellectual frills. Under fire by politicians, journalists, and ideologues, they were beaten down by the drudgery of lecture preparation, exam writing, and paper grading. Daily, they faced students who studied little and read less. Burnout hovered over their weary heads.

But I continued to see poll results reporting that faculty liked their jobs and rated themselves as above-average teachers. Hard working, unappreciated, outwardly confident, even arrogant, they privately voiced their doubts. Students were unprepared, administrators ignored the space and time required for teaching, and the public didn't understand what they were trying to do. Caught in a culture of high ideals and crass ambition, they worked in educational institutions that had evolved to recruit students and use their tuition to subsidize research. They knew teaching mattered, but so did research productivity. As one department chair expressed it: "I know I should be a better teacher and that I could be a better teacher, but I don't know where to start or where to find the time."

Having concocted a dream of a different and better mode of teaching, I had to face institutional and instructional realities that often made me feel like quitting. My vision of teaching was not only unpopular, I wasn't totally convinced it was right, and it was surely misunderstood. Over the years I have sorted and re-sorted the conflicted meanings of teaching; how we learn to teach alone and without guidance, how we end up teaching as we were taught only to rediscover the inadequacy of those approaches. Some of us innovate, find our way to other approaches, but do them with difficulty in colleges and universities designed to accommodate the ways teachers have always taught.

The conflicts that teaching provokes happen not just at an institutional level. At times during my teaching career I felt fear and anxiety. Other times I loved teaching. It dominated my thoughts and emotions, sometimes for weeks on end. I had students who shined with possibility and yet froze in performance. I saw students with wet eyes, disdainful mouths, sleeping heads, and many who faked paying attention. But what sat in front of me was the potential for lives better than my own, for worlds better than ours, and that promised potential was as crisp and enticing as my first glass of really good champagne—and just as seductive.

Teaching made me angry—those hours consumed by summaries that took all night to create and to which no one listened; stacks of awful papers to read; gut insulting examinations to grade; a stream of complaints, excuses, whining that morphed into pleading. Grandparents died, most of them during the last weeks of the course. I remember standing alone in the classroom barely holding on to the discussion's thread; holding back tears and knotting up my desire to shout profanities—maybe that would make them listen. They graduated, mostly disappeared, and if they returned as alumni, they often didn't remember my name, the course or what they had supposedly learned.

Teaching confused me. Why did I want to teach? Why bother? Was it just a ploy that allowed me to read, be always curious, make up my mind one day and change it the next? Maybe it was a way to stay a student without derision—a way not to grow up. "What is your teaching load?" teachers ask each other. It was heavy alright—endlessly evolving, interpersonally saturated, kept me awake at night, imbued with hostile barriers, and drenched with decisions. The work was never done, never got easier, and never stopped needing energy.

Teaching made me happy. Sometimes at the end of a discussion students have taken ideas where they have never been before. I helped them get there. I scored a goal, completed a concerto, put the pot roast on the table, and a moment of intense satisfaction passed through me. But then, I began preparing for the next class, and wondered if I'd ever be able to do that well again. There were momentary highs; favorite students married, I've read books some of them have written, listened to their speeches, and looked at pictures of their children. Those were my students. I can't talk about it without sounding sentimental and maybe narcissistic.

Teaching engenders an array of emotions that are often suppressed and ignored. It rests on unchallenged assumptions that make it hard to improve and even harder to change given what cognitive science now documents about learning. Before we can move to an in-depth discussion of what learning entails, we must take on the traditional approaches to teaching.

Traditional Modes of Teaching and the Cognitive Science Alternative

Two approaches underlie how we usually think, talk, write, and practice teaching. There is *teaching as performance* that connects maturing generations to the best solutions and accomplishments of the past, and there is *teaching as a didactic transmission* of culture to new generations. These visions are intertwined in the minds of most educators like rival grapevines competing for sun. They are enemies and yet accomplices. Their methods differ but they share many assumptions about the nature of knowledge, memory, learning, and life. There is a third shadowy vision infrequently assumed but sometimes evoked to remedy the shortcomings of the first two—the *coaching mode*. I'll introduce it in this chapter and explore its implications in the rest of the book.

Teaching as performing dominates the pages of alumni magazines with profiles of professors who excite, inform, and amuse. Their teaching is described with catchy phrases; such as "classroom pizzazz," "high-velocity learning," "the magic of great teaching," and "lessons alive and remembered forever." Great teachers steam into class with carts piled with props. They sport eye-slamming costumes, move to cover every inch of floor space, and radiate enthusiasm.

Sarason (1999) declares that the best teaching performers inspire the desire to learn through an artistic enactment of subject matter. Instead of force-feeding, they perform to create a hunger for learning. Professors use their understanding to ignite and guide student curiosity. What they do becomes a script that they must enact again and again with originality and passion. If teachers can't replicate the performance, Sarason (1999) argues, efforts to improve the learning process are reduced to fiddling with formulas and techniques.

Parker Palmer (1998) put it this way, "Technique is what teachers use until the real teacher arrives . . . " (p. 5). In other words, the teaching performance is carried by techniques instead of being the act of creating the conditions of learning. Enthusiasm and talent conveyed in performance transform the classroom from dead to dynamic. Performing teachers entice students to improve their minds and character. Images of this kind of teacher are the stock of education dramas from the *Dead Poets Society* to *Mr. Holland's Opus.* But there is a catch.

Sarason (1999) cautions: "Teaching is a very complicated performing art which has hardly been recognized or studied" (p. 190). That raises some interesting questions. How do we identify and select candidates, and how do we prepare them to teach? How do they gain the knowledge and skill to achieve this high art? Who are the coaches and where is the place of practice? The lack of selection and preparation of teachers become crucial obstacles when the goal is improving the educational system, argues Sarason (1999). Why don't we confront such obvious omissions? We don't select, prepare, support, and judge teachers as performing artists. We sometimes give them teaching awards, but robust, consensually determined standards aren't always used to decide who gets them. Sarason (1999) notes that we don't let just anyone become a doctor and we shouldn't allow just anyone to become a teacher.

Thrown into the classroom, the performing teacher is a lonely creature—marginally trained and almost never coached. He or she performs onstage for the intellectually immature. In college lecture halls, teachers are singularly free to teach as they see fit—each a law unto him or herself. In music, dance, and other performing arts, those who perform look to colleagues for insights on how to improve, but teachers prepare and perform solo.

As a new teacher I was both cowed and inspired by the independence. As Sarason (1999) predicted, over time I treasured the closeted freedom even as that isolation hampered my efforts to improve. In the theatre, audiences can't be ignored by performers, but not so with the students in the classroom audience. They've paid to be there whether the show is good or bad. If they decide to skip the teaching performance, they paid for it and what they miss is their loss, the teacher can argue. If the performance turns students off, that's because it demands rigor and upholds high standards. In this upside-down world, deficiencies belong to the students, not their teachers.

In learning how to teach at the Art Institute I realized that I had to be interested in students' thoughts, emotions, reactions, and suggestions. I couldn't fake it. But I didn't learn how to address the remediation they needed—the deficiencies that kept them from learning. I worked on my performance hoping that learning happened, but if it didn't at least students might be inspired if not entertained.

No one evaluated my ability to perform, offered suggestions for improvement, or provided any performance standards. Other than students, no one ever watched me. Contrast that with entry into any other performing art–take theatrical for instance. Those who act must demonstrate that they can tolerate and sustain a rigorous program of practice, can compete successfully for roles, and can perform under pressure. Most of all they must maintain a high level of creativity. That takes years, anguish, and recovery from many failures.

Imagine if new college teachers were evaluated and analyzed by the professional standards of acting. As an actor I would have been at the level of a few seasons of summer stock. I overcame my anxieties, learned my lines, and showed up on time. Maybe I had a glimmer of talent and maybe I could have gotten admitted into a program for further study, but I would have had no chance of successfully auditioning for any kind of major role. "Needs work," would be the grade my teaching performance deserved. Instead, I was judged qualified to perform at the highest level, the university classroom.

Great thespians hone their skills. Criticism helps them improve. They thrive on feedback from audiences, colleagues, and directors. Good actors seek new challenges and never cease to practice. Without similar dedication, resources, and feedback how can a performing professor improve? How, indeed, do teachers know if their performances are any good? In the long run, the academic culture's failure to recognize that criticism and collaboration are required for teaching improvement drugged me into years of complacency.

In the mythical world of academia, teaching is a different kind of performance. It's open to anyone who wants or needs to do it. It takes no special talents. It is devoid of art. It demands no training. Its craft is mysterious. Its results are miraculous. In some way beyond what psychology and common sense can explain, the knowledge of teachers directly stimulates the hearts and minds of students without any need for craft, practice, and wisdom. In the real world of university teaching, without evaluation leading to the correction of errors, improvement over time can't be expected.

And yet the prejudice among academics against teaching as performance inhibits criticism and collaboration. If you teach often and with enthusiasm, your days as a productive scholar are limited, as the administrator warned me. Some say that teaching ability degrades as the teacher ages, others that it actually erodes the teacher's cognitive functions. If teaching itself is looked down upon, then certainly watching others teach to provide feedback must be a total waste of time.

Art for most people is a mystery. Maybe the idea of teaching as an art is just a way of avoiding the problems of training and sustaining teachers. Department chairs appreciate the public relations value of performing teachers. Students flock to their courses—who doesn't love a good performance? What's not explored is how they've become creative or the extent to which these teaching performances actually promote learning.

With respect to the second common mode of teaching, the *transmission mode*, Goodlad (2004) makes the point that teachers teach as they were taught during those 16 or so years they were in school. Even though I was determined to teach differently, I started out lecturing, asking questions and judging student answers. We seem to think that just as every child walks without learning biomechanics, so anyone can teach without knowing what cognitive science says about learning. It is just a matter of imitating and new teachers have seen years' worth of examples.

What strikes education researchers such as Cuban, Gage, Goodlad, Sarason and others is the remarkable uniformity of transmission teaching across subjects, grades, schools, geography, and institutions. Typically, this process—present, question, respond—is carried out with little emotion. Goodlad (2004) adds another point. When students respond, there's an almost universal lack of corrective feedback. Rather teachers respond to student answers with more questions and then move on to the next topic. After studying schools for more than 3 decades, Sarason was struck by other uniformities. Students can't say they don't understand without seeming stupid to themselves and others. Teachers can't tell their deans, supervisors, department heads, or other instructors that they need help without seeming incompetent.

Teachers who engage in the transmission mode tell novices about something and/or show them how to do something. Students listen, then memorize and imitate what they have been told or shown. Teachers follow up with tests and grades. Thus, to learn is to memorize and demonstrate that you have memorized effectively. Learning happens through repetition enforced by rewards and punishments.

This teaching system minimizes emotions, restricts stimulation, keeps students quiet, and controls movement to maintain order in a classroom. Teachers are conduits focused on the scheduled delivery of subject matter. K–12 teachers read the scripts of other authorities; at the collegiate level professors supposedly write the scripts and then read them. Students are expected to pay attention, obey orders, and tolerate repetition.

Repetition, especially repetition without a clear and compelling end in view, is boring and stressful. The best transmission teachers are kindly, patient, and try to bolster student morale. Much like ideal parents, such teachers can make a dismal process bearable. But it's a process that enforces uniformity. In the age-graded or skill-selected classroom every student is supposed to learn the same things at about the same pace. Individual differences in curiosity, passion, or creativity get compacted by the curriculum. Since teachers must enforce standards and therefore be tough, transmitters can easily become tyrants in the mode of Washington Irving's "Ichabod Crane" or Dickens's "Mr. M'Choakumchild." The transmission mode reduces knowledge to information that can be delivered and received.

This cookbook information supposedly prepares students for adult life in the workplace, the family, community, and nation. Once memorized, it supposedly guides how students work and navigate their future social and physical worlds. The information students are given must be internalized which assumes that content is embedded in the minds of students by their teachers. Good teaching is getting more in or getting it in deeper or faster. Measure that content with dipstick tests and the system is complete.

The transmission approach assumes omniscience. The teacher must know the most important concepts, patterns, and solutions in the current culture, and what the student will need to know to thrive in the future. But in reality the teacher can't know such things. Culture changes and it can't just be transmitted. It requires interpretation and that is limited by the teacher's own experience, capacities, and biases. Anticipating the future is like making an impulsive bet. Luckily it fails, since the indelible transmission of ideas would freeze them and that would be the dystopian end of culture itself.

In terms of comprehension, retention, and transfer, the transmission model muddles along at best. As Benjamin Bloom and Associates (1956) have shown, less than 20% of students usually learn well with this approach. At best only 30% to 40% learn with add-on adaptations. Retention is low as is the ability to transfer ideas learned in one context to another. Conduits of other people's wisdom, transmission teachers don't make or expand knowledge. They just pass it on as best they can to students who don't much care about getting it. More a technical skill than an intellectual pursuit, teaching is reduced to announcing. Only scholarly research can rescue a professor from its stigma.

Whether a performing art or didactic instruction, conventional teaching is an example, like one of Rube Goldberg's immortal machines exerting maximum effort to achieve minimal results. The standard answer to all problems that result from conventional teaching is more of the same. From the teacher that means more lists, examples, and explanations and from the student more memorizing and repeating.

If more of the same is the only way a human process can be improved, then that process is simply not understood. When we do understand a process, we can set priorities. We know what is important and what is ancillary. Instead of adding more actions, we substitute new methods for ineffective ones, and we step back as needed to analyze the process from different perspectives. Above all, we understand present practices as the result of flawed human decisions, and we engage in criticism to locate their flaws and develop alternatives to overcome them.

The *coaching mode* reverses these two traditional modes and alters the instructional dynamic dramatically. According to the cognitive scientist, David Premack, teaching consists of three activities: observation, judgment, and correction. A teacher observes the novice's efforts, judges them against a standard, and intercedes to aid improvement. Students initiate the process by trying to think or act in some new way. They first need to try and necessarily fail in order for the teacher to intervene with feedback and instruction. Premack points out that while other animals imitate, only humans are capable of reversing the flow of information, so that instead of students observing teachers, teachers observe and correct students. Whereas, chimpanzee mothers never watch as their offspring try to imitate them, human mothers do. In humans, maternal feedback greatly accelerates learning. Consequently, babies learn quickly while it takes about 10 years for a chimp to figure out how to crack nuts using a rock.

Instructors can show pupils how, and the pupils may imitate, but according to the coaching mode, true learning occurs only after the pupil has tried. The teacher judges the pupil's performance and offers remedies. The student tries again and again, if necessary. The teacher can shorten the process by designing deliberate practice activities that focus student attention on what matters in the subject or skill to be learned. Just as coaches design the practice, teachers design the experiences, the students perform, and teachers then revise the design supplying more experiences or activities as needed for further practice. Then students practice until they can successfully use the skill in an actual situation.

The key then to the coaching mode is the teacher's observation of and listening to the student. Imitation, even with great effort, only produces suboptimal performances. Premack writes that imitation supplies a rough copy; coaching can polish it to an expert performance. In the nonschool world; parents, friends, colleagues, and supervisors criticize the first attempts to imitate. That helps learners improve. In the coaching teaching mode recognizing and correcting errors is key to learning.

Teachers must listen and observe to find out what students know or do not know and can or cannot do. That guides how teachers intervene and in order to intervene effectively teachers must get students to ask specific questions about their current knowledge. Lectures and discussions can't substitute for student questions, a point I hope I made in two earlier chapters. A lecturer, like a chimpanzee mother is a model, but not a teacher. The lecturer doesn't observe what students do, or how they try to apply their knowledge. Occasional quizzes, a few tests, and recitation every now and then are more like quick looks than in-depth observations of learning.

The coaching model is based on the theory that knowledge is something each learner builds for themselves. It is not something we can transmit or receive. When you know something, you are able to act on expectations and make predictions about the world around you. Knowledge consists of the generalized patterns that make prediction possible. Learning begins with doubt—the search for or formation of alternatives. It successfully ends with the creation of knowledge.

A major source of the ideas about the role of design in teaching comes from the artificial intelligence community's attempt to create intelligent machines that could function and survive in the world. Seymour Papert used that experience to critique the transmission mode of teaching which he pointed out assumes that students either get it right or get it wrong and the teacher's job is to make sure they get it right. After initial failures to build machines capable of learning, pioneers in the field like Marvin Minsky, Roger Schank, and others began to explore alternative models of learning. This creates fear of being wrong, a major obstacle to learning and teaching. Learning is a matter of isolating and correcting errors. The question to ask of students' knowledge is not whether it is right or wrong, but how it can be improved.

The downside of the coaching mode of teaching is the large amount of time and effort involved in both designing and conducting such practice.

Coaching is high risk, since failure is frequent and stressful. It requires grit, the ability to manage stress, handle pain, and take failure as a chance to improve. It necessitates the design of compelling problems and well-designed laboratories, studios, workshops, and playing spaces. It demands available experts to intercede with stories, admonitions, or principles when students fail, as they must, if they are to learn.

Most of the learning that produces the expertise of the practicing scientist, engineer, or poet is accomplished through active participation in a task which, in turn, requires teachers who can design tasks and problems and work side-by-side with students. Together they create, evaluate, improve, and apply knowledge. Students learn to be experts, and instructors hone that expertise. Ideally, the best teachers are relentlessly demanding and always striving to create better learning designs and coaching strategies.

In the coaching mode, evaluation of teaching is based on students' performances, not test scores, on applying knowledge and information to successfully solve problems in real world conditions. The preparation to teach this way requires a basic knowledge of the cognitive sciences and ideally a supervised internship of several years in designing curricula and learning to coach. I offer this not as a silver bullet but as a way to ask better questions, formulate new problems, and sharpen the dialogue of teaching practice.

The coaching teacher is: an authentic Socratic questioner of traditional certainties; an artistic performer selected, mentored, and evaluated for creativity and original improvisation; a scholar of the physiology and psychology of learning; a designer of learning spaces and moderator of disputations and debates; a coach who can design problems to guide practice; an epistemologist who understands the distinction between information and knowledge and the need to learn both in the same context; a user and developer of learning technologies; a skilled classroom researcher in the complexities of learning and teaching; a disrupter of educational dogmas and an agent of improvement; and finally a leader of the reform of higher education. And how a teacher can be all that, I will explore in the chapters that follow, written with tongue slightly in cheek.

Epilogue

I was late for class. It was already past 8. I groaned as I slipped on my topcoat. Not only was I going to be late, I had a sociologist visiting my class. She was interested in using student learning teams in the several introductory courses she taught. She asked to sit in to see a demonstration. I was happy to have her. I was jogging now, but still going to be at least 10 minutes late. My legs ached; my mouth sucked wind. I banged the door open and arrived, panting with a bright pink face. And nothing happened.

The students were arranged in their clusters, making the room look like a disorderly fraternal banquet. The air buzzed with conversations; I heard arguments, explanations, critiques. The visiting professor sat busily taking notes. I walked to the instructor's desk in the supposedly front of the room, shed my coat, grabbed my notes for the day, and turned to watch. No one paid any attention. It was as if I wasn't there. Heart thumping. I walked over to the visitor. "I'm sorry. I got delayed. Do you want to come another time?"

She looked up either amused or annoyed, I couldn't tell. "It's fine," she said. "It's a wonderful demonstration. Most of them were here before the period began. They asked me who I was, I explained, and they excused themselves to get to work on your assignments. It was like you said. They seemed to like to learn. They were eager to get to work."

I surveyed the class again. Yes, I was proud. With me or without they had plunged into the work of the day without prodding. But an insistent voice was banging in my head, "They didn't even notice I was . . . They didn't even see me bounce into the room. I'm invisible, unnecessary, and out of a job."

At that moment a disagreement exploded in the far corners of the room—yells of "Wrong! Wrong!" "He didn't say that." "It's inconsistent." "What?" "It fits. It fits." I tacked across the room around jammed desk seats, over backpacks, as I made my way toward the noisy team. Arriving I hesitated. "Sit down, sit down," they beckoned. "We're in trouble. We need your help."

References

Bloom, B. & Associates. (1956). *Taxonomy of educational objectives.* Longman, Green and Co.

Goodlad, J. I. (2004). *Romances with schools: A life of education.* McGraw Hill.

Palmer, P. J. (1998). *The courage to teach: Exploring the inner landscape of a teacher's life.* Jossey-Bass.

Sarason, S. B. (1999). *Teaching as a performing art.* Teachers College Press.

7

WHAT IS LEARNING?

Much of what has preceded has focused on teaching, especially how so many current approaches to teaching and assumptions about education do not foster the learning goals we aspire to achieve. A better understanding of what's happening in the brain when we learn makes even clearer why teaching so often fails to motivate learning. It also makes it easier to understand the kind of changes that need to be made. Current developments in neuroscience reveal more than we previously knew about how the brain is structured and the functional implications of that structure. Both brain architecture and operation determine how we learn which has all sorts of implications for how we teach. Not everything we know about brains and learning is easily understood, especially in light of the prevailing assumptions about both, but examples help, and so I have decided to launch this exploration of how brains learn using my experiences learning to read.

Learning to Read

Fun With Dick and Jane wasn't. His finger traced the letters as he repeated the words: "Come, Dick. Come and see. Come, come. Come and see. Come and see Spot." Dick was a boy. Spot was a dog. Jane was speaking. Their lives were filled with pictures and a few words. The teacher rapped her pointer on the desk to conduct the boring recital. Students mouthed the words in unison. Then each in turn stood and said the words again.

She pointed to him, "Larry." He frowned. She fired, "Larry."

Disgust shot through him. He shouted from his seat: "Come, come, come, come. See, see, see, see, see. Spot, spot, spot, spot, spot . . . "

"Enough. You're not reading, you are just repeating sounds."

His eyes flashed at the truth. The class giggled. Swiftly rousted to a solitary chair in the corner, he clutched the awful book and used his anger to douse his tears. "School was a . . . " he tried to think of the worst expletive he knew. In real books, beyond letters and words there was a world he desired. It was a world of lovely Heidi, milk, and cheese. There lived brave tailors, stubborn ducks, lumbering giants, frogs to kiss, and witches to escape. It was also a world of George Washington, Pecos Bill, and Hereward the Wake. He entered that world each bedtime when his parents read to him. For him, the whole point of going to school was to travel in time and space, and enter the lives of warriors, ogres, and proud losers. But the dreadful Dick and Jane blocked the way. Why couldn't he just read a real book?

In school he hated reading. He learned the alphabet and memorized lists of words well enough to pass into third grade. By that time he was adept at avoiding school books. His worst challenge was the library reading period. For 50 minutes he was supposed to select a book and quietly read it. Convinced there were no books in the big room he wanted to read, he tried to find the shortest book on the shelves. His father had given him a ruler that he decided to use to measure the spines.

Mrs. Witherspoon looked bookish with her brown hair dusted grey, feet shod in flats, and torso decked with careless cardigans. She usually read or held a book with a finger to mark her page as she patrolled the room. The school librarian, she made and enforced rules, managing to both intimidate and welcome each new class of readers into the library.

"And where is your book, young man?" asked Mrs. Witherspoon.

"Gonna get it."

He wandered around the room's book-lined walls trying to look studious. In a section of Disney titles, he found one about Pluto, Mickey's banana-yellow dog. The spine measured 3/8 of an inch. It was short. He tucked the slim volume under his arm and turned to be blocked by the librarian's green wool sweater.

"Class, class" she chimed. "Look at Larry. He's used a ruler to find a very thin book." She continued, "Never have I ever seen such sloth. Here he is, Larry the lazy. Now, you take that teeny-weeny first grade book back to your table and try to read it!"

He stiff-stepped back to the table to brush through Pluto's pages. Classmates watched. The librarian kept him in her sights. Seething, he returned Pluto to the shelf and stalked the walls of books. She was over his shoulder in an instant. "Now what are you doing?"

"I am finding a big book."

"You are, are you? And what will you do with your big book?"

"Read it."

"Really? Let's see? Over here. These are the new books and some are big and thick."

The thickest was green and titled *The Wright Brothers: A Biography*. He didn't know who the Wright brothers were. He didn't know what a biography was. But she was watching him. Determined to make her wrong, he grabbed the book and headed back to the table. The first full page was impossible. There were words he knew—both, were, father, others, brothers, do, with, gift, spin, had—but there were long strange words he didn't—mechanical, gyroscope, and punctually. He flipped on; the whole book was like that. His palms heated. How was he going to read this book? He glanced at the librarian. She watched him with a new smile as if to say, "Now I've got you!" He glared back. Her sea hag smile inspired him. With nothing to lose he attacked the words with his Thimble Theater methods. He sounded out a few words, then "enthusiasm" loomed. He broke it down to "en" "thus" "issem."

Then he remembered the rule: If you found a word you didn't know you could take your book to Mrs. Witherspoon and she would help. Up he walked to her desk and pointed to the word and mumbled his sounds and asked what it meant. Her look was quizzical, maybe suspicious, but she took the volume. She corrected his sounds until he could say "enthusiasm."

"That's a big word. Do you know what it means?"

"Fun?" he guessed.

She chuckled, "More like excitement—to be excited about doing something. Could you be excited about airplanes?"

"Yes," his smile slipped out, "I am." He spun and carried the Wrights back to his seat.

That was the procedure. He would find the words he knew and sound out the words he didn't, and then carry the book to the librarian, who corrected his pronunciation and discussed the meaning. Five times he repeated the sequence until the period ended. He left, sure he could harass the librarian with words and questions for the rest of the semester.

Almost accidentally he deciphered the story. When Orville Wright was sent to kindergarten, he lost interest the first day. After that he would leave the house for school, but instead he went to a friend's house where they took apart an abandoned sewing machine. In the afternoon he came home as expected. He did this for several weeks before his mother stopped at school and his teacher said she hadn't seen him since the first day. Pleased that Orville didn't like school, he loved the story.

In the next library class he pressed on, wrestling with sounds, letters, and words. Sounding out "sprocket, chain, and wheel" delighted him. These were garage and farm words—not the prissy words of Dick and Jane. The pages were like talking to uncles or his father. At times he would meet a word like "omit." He could say it, but he didn't know it. At Mrs. Witherspoon's desk he pointed to the word on the page and their routine began, but this time it ended differently.

"Come here," she moved toward a wall of high windows at the end of the room and pointed to a stupendous (a word he just discovered) book.

"This is a dictionary, where you can find the meaning of any word. It works like this." She demonstrated as she led him to "omit." "That's a definition. Can you read that?"

"Le . . . ave out, not in . . . insert."

"Insert—guess the meaning."

"Put."

"Good guess."

And so it went letter after letter, word after word, sentence after sentence, page after page, and guess after guess. As he progressed, she pointed out diacritical marks so he could take an unknown word directly to the dictionary, sound it out, try a meaning, and check that against the dictionary's usage. Now the reading went faster. He could escape to the sandy hills of the North Carolina shore lying next to Wilbur Wright as the fragile glider slid down the rails into the wind. He forgot to hate Mrs. Witherspoon and school. The book opened a grown-up world to navigate. He rewrote the story of his life—no more a budding Popeye, no more a brave tailor who would show them, no longer the disguised frog who was really a prince. When grown-ups asked him what he wanted to be when he grew up he said "aeronautical engineer."

Reading is an extraordinary mental feat. According to neuroscientist, Stanislas Dehaene (2009), any reader can select a meaning out of 50,000 possible words in tenths of a second based on a few light strokes on their retinas (2009, p. 42). Readers are not aware of the decisions and intricacies this requires. Not everyone remembers how they learned to read, but fluency seems to come all at once and is self-taught. Learning to read depends more on desire than intelligence. Precocious children read by age 4 without teaching. Before compulsory schooling most people learned to read at home with minimal instruction. In 1860 almost two thirds of the population of the United States (including slaves) were literate. Reading is only a few thousand years old, so it can't be a product of evolution. It is, as Dehaene writes, a human invention adapted to the brain's structure. Reading is a perfect place to start the quest to better understand the role the brain plays in learning.

What Is Learning Anyway?

Learning is a puzzle. We spontaneously learn names, landmarks, faces, recipes, and even trivia. Other things are learned unconsciously like shapes, edges, colors, distance, musical harmonies, and our native speech. We seem to know the difference between living and dead objects, how other minds work, the time of day or night, and causality without any learning at all. We learn skills through practice like throwing baseballs, playing violins, writing essays, and creating arguments. We say we learn from experience when we frequently don't, as hangovers attest.

We use the word all the time, never thinking we're confused about what it means, but ask "What is learning?" and then Google it. You'll get more than one trillion entries. More learning, deep learning, rote learning, rich learning, active learning, passive learning, meaningful learning, lasting learning, overlearning, or the transfer of learning. We use all of these terms assuming we know what we're talking about when in fact these many adjectives connected to learning are clues to our confusion.

Artificial intelligence pioneer, Marvin Minsky (2006) says that the word "learning" creates unnecessary ignorance by appearing to have meaning when it has none. That leads us, says Minsky, to use the word without thought or analysis—we don't try to understand it. And for most of human history we did not have the information or the language to investigate or to fathom the human mind and brain. It was not until the advent of computers and computer science that we acquired new perspectives and analytical tools to consider what happens in the brain when it's learning.

Learning takes place in the brain. If we could jam all the wires, switches, generators, and transformers plus all the electrical and electronic devices in the world into a 5-gallon bucket that would not approach the level of the brain's complexity. The 3-pound human brain contains an estimated 85 billion neurons, more than 100 trillion synapses, around 80 billion glial cells, and over 100,000 miles of insulated nerve fibers. To get a sense of its magnitude consider that there are one thousand times more synapses in the brain than there are stars in the universe. (See Suzana Herculano-Houzel 2016). Human brains are products of half a billion years of evolution and do not lend themselves to simple descriptions or explanations. We need to create more complex ways to describe them and explain how they work.

However, the simpler we take learning to be the more enigmatic it becomes. We end up with definitions that include any process that in living organisms leads to permanent capacity change and which is not solely due to biological maturation or ageing; or, put it more concisely, learning is "lots of stuff." To avoid vapidity, we also need to create more entangled stories and intricate theories to explain learning, but that's not how my thinking about learning started.

Originally, I thought that humans learned by absorbing the wisdom of their cultures and then used testing to further develop their understanding of it. In earlier times humans learned without being taught. Over time teaching became a necessary practice as cultures became more elaborate, complex, and specialized. But as the years of my teaching career started adding up, the connection between teaching and learning remained a confounding puzzle. I could teach and sometimes my students would learn and sometimes they did not. When they failed to learn, which was often, I wanted to know why and what I could do about it.

One of the first places I looked in my quest to better understand learning was the explanation offered by the associationist-behaviorists. The mind, the behaviorists believed, was a blank slate or an empty vessel. In their terms, learning was the formation of habits. Thorndike's law of effect states that in a given situation, if something desirable results from an action, that action will be associated with the situation. If the sequence is repeated often enough, then whenever the learner encounters the same situation the same actions are more likely. If the actions don't have pleasing consequences, then those actions are less likely to occur. This means the best conditions for learning are those in which the learner can respond, repeat the response often, and perceive a reward. Since repetitions strengthen associations, drill is the best way to form habits.

A lot of teachers try to promote learning using behaviorist approaches. They evaluate and reward the right responses and provide enough cues that students make few mistakes. Mistakes are bad since they might become habits. The promise of behaviorist education is that eventually in high school, college, graduate school, or a profession there will be opportunities for the student to apply the content and use it to learn more. But none of that can happen before the right habits and foundational knowledge are in place.

However, as many of us who teach have discovered, delaying real learning tasks until content basics have been memorized depresses motivation. It means struggling to memorize material that appears to be irrelevant and of little interest. Despite this formula for failure, behaviorist assumptions dominate much of the language and routines of learning. We all seem to believe that if we reward behavior it will become habit. This dog training approach is how we get our children to clean up their rooms. But wait, most children don't clean up their rooms. And my students weren't learning.

Minsky (1988) points out that animals usually do things one way and if the environment prevents them from doing it, then the animals die. Our resourcefulness lies in the many alternative representations of reality available to us. When one way of looking at the situation leads to a dead end, we can try something else. Rarely do we do anything in just one way. Watch people wash dishes or load a dishwasher. I happen to know the best way to do both, but even close family members insist on doing it differently. In this spirit, Minsky argues that there isn't going to be a concise set of basic propositions that explain thinking, learning, seeing, or remembering. We need to generate a great variety of ideas about learning to gain a handle on how it works. Behaviorism was not a story that made sense to me—it didn't explain why my students weren't learning.

Finding My Way to the Cognitive Revolution

J. Z. Young (1960) has written about a rare form of blindness at birth that can be corrected later by surgery. What would a newly sighted patient see? In numerous cases the results were the same: The patient's eyes opened to a painful spinning mass of lights and colors. Like someone faced with their first abstract painting, they could see only meaningless shapes and smears of colors. Many of the patients responded with anger. The visual world made no sense. Overwhelmed, they lapsed into behaving as though they were still blind.

Why couldn't patients see if their eyes were functioning properly? Young (1960) wrote that they had not learned the rules of seeing. "We are not conscious that there are any such rules; we think that we see, as we say, 'naturally'. But we have in fact learned a whole set of rules during childhood" (p. 62). He went on to point out that not having learned those rules, people can't select stimuli to fit our models of shape, color, and movement. For all intents and purposes, they can't see.

Young's observations suggested that vision is not the result of a set of genetic rules locked in our brains but requires sorting through stimuli in order to make sense of the external world. That contradicted something I had believed for years. I thought the brain observed the world and recorded what it saw. Instead, I learned, the brain assembles stimuli into what cognitive psychologists refer to as a "representation," which can be defined as a picture or map of what reality looks like. The idea that the brain represents the world and that those representations are all that we know about reality made me question my prior understanding.

Wanting to learn more about the "rules of seeing," I stumbled across a work by E.C. Tolman (1966). In the early 20th century, researchers in animal learning thought the brain worked something like a telegraph exchange where stimuli were connected to responses. Through a series of ingenious experiments Tolman demonstrated that rats in mazes actively searched for general environmental patterns rather than rewards. They formed, in his terms, cognitive maps—sets of expectations about the dynamic world or those representations. These maps changed the animal's perceptions, memories, and inferences about the future. They guided the ways the rats performed.

Rats that were allowed to explore the maze before their learning trials had broader, more detailed maps than hungry rats that learned the maze determined to get food. The broader maps contained not only the rules of the correct path, but also the general orientation of the maze which the rats had discovered during that early exploration. When the experimenters changed the mazes, rats with broad maps quickly found a new path to the reward. The hungry rats simply repeated what was now a false trail, gave up, or became enraged. Tolman concluded that the quality of the rats' representations depended on the conditions under which they learned. But Tolman's (1966) more significant insight was that, just as the narrowing of cognitive maps created learning dysfunctions in rats, it also could do so in humans. He reasoned that human learning disabilities—repetitions of failure, frozen confusion, or angered resistance—could be caused by faulty environments.

That idea made sense in terms of students' previous educational experiences. They sat in hard seats absorbing predigested "facts" out of context and under threat of failure, and that resulted in narrow cognitive maps. Classrooms full of problems, noisy controversies, questions, and mistakes could promote complex broad maps. Narrow maps made further learning difficult, even distasteful. Broad maps invited learning.

I started to understand why students resisted my approaches to teaching. I wanted them to explore and try things; they had learned to follow the correct paths laid down by teachers who wanted to keep them from making mistakes. Clearly, I could not foster development of broad maps by requiring them. Students had to try out their own ideas, to doubt and explore. But like those formerly blind patients, my students already had their rules and maps based on years of experience in school. The approach I was taking wasn't on their maps and therefore did not exist. Like the rats, they were lost and frustrated.

Learners already have a myriad of beliefs that constitute their a priori common sense. In Young's (1960) terms these are the learner's certainties—rules of seeing, sensing, feeling, hearing, and thinking. In Tolman's (1966) terms they are expectations produced by cognitive maps. Learners can change the rules and their cognitive maps, but learners can't live without mapping reality. Just as the brain must have rules to see, so it must have rules to think and it must map the world to do either. This further explains what Young means when he says the brain represents the world but does not record it. I began to see that I could not change students' minds, but I could enable them to change their representations. So began my cognitive revolution, which was a way of understanding learning that made sense to me.

Noam Chomsky (1966), the linguist and philosopher, rattled the intellectual world in the 1950s and 1960s by arguing that a reliable account of how knowledge is created (read, how people learn) would require understanding the innate architecture of the mind. For Chomsky, the mind doesn't duplicate the noise of the world; it sorts and selects what helps it survive. For example, infants pick from the noise around them the sounds and rhythms that are language related. If we paid attention to the deluge of sensations that bombard us, we would go mad. Chomsky forcefully argued that the mind is structured to act as a filter.

The cognitive revolution recognizes that the key to understanding learning is knowing how the mind is structured and operates. And that understanding of learning must be based on theoretical proposals, experiments, and the investigations of brain physiology. It's an ongoing revolution, often derailed, but we live in its exciting promise of new avenues of research in psychology, linguistics, neurosciences. Bottom line: The cognitive revolution offers one of those entangled stories and intricate theories of how learning works based on how the brain is structured and functions.

Natural Learning: Doing It My Way

Esther Thelen and Linda Smith (1994) note that individual differences pose a challenge for our understanding of learning. I learned to read by doing a Sinatra—I did it "my way." I resisted and sabotaged school because how I was being taught collided with my instincts to learn. Students do learn in many different ways. Human brains are more unique than fingerprints. As a teacher I never found a teaching practice that worked for everyone. Yet we treat differences in how students learn as trivial or extraneous. Or we try to capsulize those differences into general categories of "learning styles," misunderstanding that the variation in how students learn is fundamental to human innovation and creativity.

J. Scott Armstrong (2010), a maverick professor of marketing at the Wharton School, calls these individual approaches to learning "natural learning." According to him, when people set objectives, break them into tasks, and then compare the results with intentions and make corrections as needed, they learn. My learning blossomed in the third grade when I set my goals and devised tasks in reading. I retrieved, inferred, guessed, crashed, recovered, and reveled in my new powers. I didn't get criticized when I failed to read a sentence or understand a page. No one quizzed me on Orville's education or how old Wilbur was. There were no grades. Mrs. Witherspoon noted my progress with a nod. I took responsibility for learning.

From birth, kids are breathtaking learners. They organize the myriad sensations of life into shapes, sounds, tastes, and sensations. They intrepidly fail and persist until they learn. They spontaneously apply their nascent knowledge of the world and revise it. So adept are infants at learning that they seem to absorb information without effort. We now know that is an illusion. Baby brains are selective and respond to specific stimuli—faces, voices, words, and shapes. They explore and learn the world almost like instinctual scientists. They generalize instantly, act on those generalizations and when their expectations fail, they revise the general pattern.

Like many of you, I have seen infant learning firsthand. I remember one day when my son Duncan was just able to pull himself up to toddle. Bare chested and diapered, he lurched around the living room on rubbery legs. He looked like a miniature sumo wrestler with more enthusiasm than skill. Ignoring me, Duncan attacked the room with intensity—touching, pushing, and grasping. He reached for the television, rocked off balance, and grabbed the big black knob, accidentally twisting it. Boom. The screen filled and sound shook the room. He sat back on his ever-ready bottom; looked at me and started to cry, then stopped and pulled up to focus on the knob, grasping and turning it as the sound blared or died and the picture vanished and reappeared. He delighted in this for a few minutes and then scanned the room looking for another knob. There on a closet door, he saw it and dropped to his knees, crawled over, pulled up and struggled to grasp and turn the knob with two hands. The door swung open sending him once again to his backside. His face registered pain, consternation, delight, and determination. He explored the house and within two days he located and manipulated every knob in the house—he learned knobs. These memories flooded my mind with joy. This was what it was once like to learn.

This "drive to learn" prefigures our education. To say it is our most important instinct is no exaggeration. Even with all its demands—trials, failures, and close attention to getting hands, feet, and eyes in the right positions—this learning is joyous. Each child does it in his or her own unique way. No two babies learn to walk in the same way. Some crawl first, some scoot, some roll, and some start walking all at once. Since nearly all infants achieve the same levels of competence, it is easy to miss their uniqueness.

Joy and freedom hide the purposefulness of play, but if it's interrupted, the child resists. Exploring, explaining, and learning are children's goals. How they accomplish those goals is unique, but it's not learning for the faint-hearted. Childhood play is a demanding taskmaster—intense, varied, demanding, and continuous. As Minsky (2006) observes in *The Emotion Machine,* never again will anything drive learners to work as hard. It makes classrooms look like cognitive retirement homes.

No One Has to Teach the Brain How to Learn

In the past 30 years as part of the cognitive revolution, psychologists like Alison Gopnik (2003) and others have used video cameras to record the reactions of babies and to test a series of hypotheses about infant minds. They found that their minds are innately structured to learn in precise ways. Gopnik's "theory theory" would interpret my son Duncan's adventures as hypothesis testing—"turning knob things makes stuff happen." His experiments generated a variety of outcomes—many failures and some successes. He quickly created a category "knobs" which he could use to guide his actions.

In this view children don't absorb information; they chase and grab it from the barrage of stimuli they face. Gopnik emphasizes that children explore based on theories that enable them to anticipate and predict. When they act on those theories, they make or don't make things happen. In either case they generate relevant information that can confirm or discredit their theories. If alternative theories are better at anticipating, predicting, and deciding, they replace the earlier ones.

Babies conjure more alternatives and they revise their representations more frequently than adults do. That is what learning is about—changes in mental representations, adjusting those maps of reality. Those changes can be reaffirmation, refutation, slight adjustments, or major overhaul. Such changes require imagination and toddlers' imaginations start working as early as 18 months once they grasp causality. Then they can conceive new ways to manipulate and anticipate their environment. A child's mental life is busy and complex. Gopnik (2003) describes it like being in love, in Paris, and walking down the street after two double shots of espresso.

We might say then that the brain has evolved to learn, like the body has evolved to walk and run, eyes to configure the world into shapes, colors, and movements, and stomachs to digest food. No one teaches bodies, eyes, and stomachs to do these things. Similarly, the brain knows how to learn without anyone teaching it. Almost everyone begins life as a great learner, without being taught, and almost always outside of school confines.

This research exploring how infants learn (and I'm skittering across the surface of what's been discovered) raises some disturbing questions. If the human brain is built to learn, why do so many children slog through school? Why does the joy of learning evaporate when children become students? Why do students gradually quit asking questions, generating hypotheses, and experimenting? Why are so many adults ignorant in important ways?

I regularly encountered this joyless learning in my classrooms: well-planned assignments but poor outcomes, good discussions leading to poor decisions, well-crafted lectures with little impact, laboriously corrected assignments never picked up, team assignments sliced into individual tasks, assigned readings ignored, and the frequent decline in interest, judgment, and competence as students approach graduation. I couldn't explain what happened or answer the questions student behavior raised.

Great learning happens when a student bolts into her proximal zone of ignorance and becomes productively stupid; accepts that her current view of the world is mistaken or inadequate in some ways and believes she can fix it. As with Galileo when he recognized that he didn't understand falling objects, productive stupidity forces students to fall back on their natural learning techniques. They don't act like infants, but they do become curious, ask, and try to answer their own questions. This is the way we all learn in life and on the job when we are confronted with our ignorance. We formulate problems to solve—like how to a write a book on mistaken habits of teaching—and we struggle to do what is necessary to solve them.

Education from kindergarten to college assumes that learning requires ardent teaching. Learning is supposedly onerous and foreign to students' natural inclinations. Teachers must motivate students, instill them with a desire to learn, train them in basic intellectual skills, and discipline them until they learn to follow the rules. Given what the cognitive revolution has documented about infant learning, how can that be true? Is learning something that must be forced upon children who look like they were born loving to learn?

The cognitive scientists, Scott Atran and Dan Sperber (1991) note that in some societies children become competent adults without schools or designated teachers. They learn by observation, imitation, play, and apprenticeships. Parents and adults demonstrate some skills and recount lore as by-products of other activities. Adults seem instinctively to help youngsters learn. They not only pick them up and wipe tears, they explain mistakes, suggest alternatives, and show them how.

However, in Western societies learning and teaching are so conflated that when youngsters demonstrate cultural literacy, we assume they have been taught. The rule is where there is learning, there must have been teaching. Even when there are no teachers, we still assume teaching, and we say experience taught us or we taught ourselves. If college students have picked up some skills, attitudes, and information, we assume they were taught. Too often we overlook what's being learned outside of school. It's not part of how we talk about education and what people have learned, even though we all recognize that people can learn without any teaching and they can be taught without much learning.

According to the anthropologist, David Lancy, the notion that young children need to be taught is quite recent and provincial. In the Western world, parents equate child-rearing with teaching—mostly by parents but also by caregivers, coaches, and classroom teachers. In contrast, Lancy's surveys of a variety of cultures throughout history lead him to conclude that "Teaching—even if defined, minimally, as self-conscious demonstration—is rare in the accounts of anthropologists and historians . . . " (p. 97). Rather than a common necessity, teaching has been the exception in human history. Anthropological studies of child-raising throughout the world show that children learn their cultures largely without instruction. In most non-industrial societies children watch, imitate, and play. They learn adult skills by practicing tasks like hunting, cooking, or farming by using cast-off or miniature tools. This kind of learning results in a complex and extensive knowledge of the world that we call common sense.

As human beings we are remarkable learners. We make do under the most absurd political regimes and poorly designed organizations. We explore and adapt to extreme and toxic environments like outer space. We do this by assembling patterns of causal connections. We build representations based on those connections, act on them, experimentally or in play, thereby discerning their limits and potentials. This enables us to adapt and change the environment to improve our quality of life. This ability to direct, test, and correct experience with theories makes human learning distinctive. Teachers do have a role to play and it can be a more effective role. But it begins with the recognition that brains do not need teachers in order to learn.

Evolution, Brain Development, and Learning

Evolution has played a role in brain development. The tasks and hazards of millennia of years shaped the human brain. During that time humans lived in small bands, hunting and gathering for survival. Their brains grew in size and complexity when these early humans had to act and react with little and unreliable information. Anthropologists find that the remnants of hunter–gatherer societies today have large but relatively superficial understanding of their world beyond what survival demands (Atran, 1990).

Early human brains had to solve the problems of grubbing for roots, searching for berries, and killing animals twice their size. Today this inherited brain formulates and solves a range of complex problems in mathematics, cosmology, quantum gravity, immunology, and bridge building. It seems as though there's an immense distance between these early brains and the amazing brain of someone like Sir Isaac Newton. He didn't worry about hunting, eating, or shelter. His vision of the cosmos was abstract, mathematical, and astonishingly accurate, revealing relationships unavailable to the human senses. Is the same brain capable of tracking beasts and mapping the barely visible elements of the solar system?

Louis Liebenberg (1990) writes that "The art of tracking is one of the most fundamental and universal factors in hunting" (p. 24). Our ancestors had primitive weapons; sharp stones, pointed sticks, plus puny bows and arrows. Their bodies were not powerful or swift. To hunt often was to persistently trail, wear down, and kill their food at close quarters.

Tracking depends on an uncanny ability to think about what cannot be seen and artfully guess about what might be going on. The recognition of tracks and what they infer about the conditions and intentions of prey takes skill and imagination. The hunter needs to know where the animals seek food, drink, find mates, or rest in safety. He must infer the beast's age, sex, condition, and even intentions from the marks it makes in passing. The landscape may contain features that block or accommodate animal movements. Hunter must think like the beast. How fast is it moving and in what direction? If the animal isn't where the hunter anticipated, he must discard or alter what he thought would happen and set a new ambush.

In sum, successful early hunters created *representations* (those maps, pictures, models, and stories) of the lives of their prey in order to creatively anticipate their behavior. The hunter's guesses got critiqued, tested, and improved by the hunting band. Liebenberg (1990) asserts that tracking is similar to the way a physicist tracks unseen particles. Physicists represent or have developed understandings of how particles behave in the subatomic world. They create hypotheses based on those models, and then test them against observations. Similarly, mathematicians start with a conscious guess that they explore until they can state clearly the assumptions that led to it. Then they must defend their conjectures against the best critiques of colleagues.

Anthropologists missed the cognitive complexity of tracking because they had not witnessed it. Fortunately, this million-year-old tradition was investigated only a few years before it ended. In 1990, Liebenberg accompanied hunters in a hunt that involved running down a Kudu bull. The hunters tried to dissuade him from joining the hunt and he almost died during it. (See the account in Liebenberg, 2013, chapter 2). During that experience Liebenberg discovered the complexities involved in tracking. He equated what successful tracking required to the intellectual capacities needed to understand modern math and physics.

But a different understanding of brain development dominates our views of education. According to David Geary (1995), the evolutionary psychologist, the innate abilities of the brain are necessary but not sufficient for advanced scientific thinking. The classroom separates "knowing what" (the content) from "knowing how" (applying the content). "Knowing what" is considered sufficient, even when that knowledge is independent of context and has never been used. It does make transfer from instructor to student easier since it avoids the questions, criticism, and the failures required to produce knowledge reliable enough to guide action. In the living world knowing and doing are inseparable; in school they are divorced which hampers teaching and learning.

An interesting paradox grows out of educators' understandings of the role evolution plays. The extensive remodeling of the mind required to support academic achievement must start with and build on what the hunter-gatherer knows. In this view, children's brains have evolved to acquire a vast amount of commonsense knowledge that guides them through life, but this knowledge supposedly blocks the reception of academic content. If knowledge is to advance, according to this view of education, then brains must be trained in school to accept truths—generalizations that cannot be questioned, critiqued, or tested. This transmission approach goes against every basic learning practice—to question, imagine, critique, and apply—because the human brain, as it has evolved, is not suited to absorbing decontextualized abstract content. What's the use of knowing something you have no opportunity to use?

When instructors strive to present clear, well-organized content to brains that thrive on questions, ambiguity, and doubt they promote a cognitive war. Students fight back by playing along with what's required. They seek right answers, cheat, and cram for exams. If they happen to get curious or want to learn something, they are forced into various forms of subversion or rebellion. The more they like to learn—and our discussion of infant learning shows that everyone does—the more they don't like school.

Those who think students' brains are capable of academic pursuits note that to become an expert in biology, Shakespeare, or astronomy means the student must master the accumulated knowledge in those fields, become initiated into the appropriate community of scholars, and be able to work with high-tech equipment and analytical methods. Scholars, be they scientists or liberal artists, require structured communities of practice and criticism. Scholars who believe the inherited brain capacities aren't enough to facilitate unaided learning, point out the errors of commonsense assumptions. Those must be corrected—the mental slate must not only be wiped, it has to be recast in some new form; abstract and free of living contexts.

No one denies that a body of knowledge must be mastered. But the crux is how you gain that mastery. Can students build their own views to accommodate current knowledge or do they have to submit to the assumed truth of that knowledge and restate it on demand? Ultimately, when they are no longer students but professionals, they must evaluate and use that knowledge on their own. We all know that you don't get ahead in life by passing multiple-choice tests or writing papers.

What happens when we teach by transmission? I have already written about the physics education reform movement and the documentation that introductory courses taught in the "let me tell you about Newtonian mechanics" format result in remarkably small gains in student understanding (Hake, 1998; Mazur, 2009). The iconoclast of the classroom, John Gatto (2000) notes that children appropriately resist teaching but not learning.

This discussion of brain structure and learning has been long and meandering, but it ends with straightforward conclusions. Evolution has given us brains spectacularly developed for learning and that learning, even when it's complex, can take place without teachers. In fact, when teachers get involved, problems frequently emerge. Educators assume that what students have learned is limited and must be recast and rebuilt to accommodate academic learning. Unfortunately, they try to make corrections with methods that are the antithesis of how brains are structured to learn.

Is the Brain Selective or Instructive?

To survive, an organism or system has to fit into its environment. We see this all around us in animal species, cells, organs, individuals, and institutions. This ability to fit could be evidence for a grand design, if not a grand designer. It could suggest that fitting in is a product of instruction. Or, it could imply that adaptive systems are selective. They proceed through trials, errors, and corrections, generating blind variations that succeed to some extent or come to nothing. In evolution, Darwin's theory explained how different species adapt to environmental changes. New conditions make it likely (but don't guarantee) that some inherited traits will be crucial for survival and others will not. Organisms with such traits will outbreed others, that is, the conditions "select" from genetic features those that contribute to survival. However, our dominant stories about human learning are still instructive. Education tries to make changes—figuratively rewire—the brain.

Learning changes the physical structure of the brain and those structural changes alter the functional organization or simply "learning organizes and reorganizes the brain" (Branford et al., 1999, p. 115). David Sousa (2006) declares "Educators are the only profession whose job it is to change the human mind every day" (p. 10). This way of thinking about the brain and learning rests on the assumption that learning is a single simple process common to all animals and humans with the architecture of the brain contributing little.

Some cognitive scientists disagree. Gallistel and King (2009) explain that "Learning is the extraction from experience of information about the state of the world, which information is carried forward in memory to inform subsequent behavior." I interpret that to mean that the brain begins with architecture that is the product of eons of evolution. Its structure has evolved to respond to a world that changes. In educational terms, brains begin with knowledge.

Consider the immune system: It works as a selective system. Immunologists, as you might guess, had a difficult time accepting that. Initially, they believed that all specific antibodies were generated by an instructive process. Antigens from outside impressed their shapes onto the organism's molecules, which flagged them for antibodies that killed them. That's not what they discovered. Instead, organisms generate repertoires of many millions of specific antibodies. Those repertoires are so huge that every possible antigen shape entering an organism will encounter at least one antibody that can recognize and label it for destruction. Today immunologists accept that organisms utilize this selective system.

The immunology case shows how we can improve our understanding when we challenge conventional assumptions. It opens opportunities to approach the brain as something different than an efficient but somehow moldable machine. Cognitive and neuroscientists (such as Changeux, 1995; Dehaene, 2009; Piatelli-Palmarini, 1989) think that selective hypotheses are the best way to investigate the brain.

In neuroscience selective theories focus on the developing organization and functionality of brain structures in response to sensory signals never encountered before. The brain confronts an ever-changing environment and it selects from a preexisting diverse repertoire of internal representations. When those representations or models repeatedly fail to explain what's happening in the environment, they're rejected. But those models, maps, or narratives that solve or help to solve problems are selected. Selective systems constantly generate a variety of internal representations. They're what we have on hand before any experience happens to us. In the same way infants reach, taste, and gaze, selective systems guide interactions with the environment.

The mechanisms of a selective system are blind variation, selection, and transmission. *Blind variation* means that we conjecture about what might work without knowing whether it will work. The environment in which the brain functions changes. Our knowledge consists of representations and theories about the past that haven't yet been fully tested or criticized. They are imperfect and subject to criticism and refinement. In contrast, the instructive view inductively derives the future from the past. Although this is logically impossible, it seems psychologically compelling. It implies that if we adroitly accumulate and organize information about the world, we can formulate an understanding of the future, which of course we cannot.

I find the case for brains as selective systems compelling. I return to how I learned to read, "And so it went letter after letter, word after word, sentence after sentence, page after page, and guess after guess." Mrs. Winterspoon played an important role, but she did not teach me to read. She did not instruct me. I learned to read when I tried to use what I knew (a few words) to understand a book that contained all sorts of words I didn't know. My understanding of how to read failed—I couldn't read. I tried alternatives, including some offered by Mrs. Winterspoon. Some of what I tried failed, some things worked. I was in the process of revising, recreating my representation of reading, and it was a selective process.

Principles for Learning and Implications for Teaching

If the human brain is a selective system, as by now you know I think it is, then these principles of learning follow:

1. Learning is a process of eliminating useless representations and correcting and improving those that prove useful. "Programs are assembled by selecting from the vast number of possibilities that are available and then increasing the reliability of the chosen actions." (Young, 1979, p. 812).
2. Learning begins with wildly variable efforts that become organized through deliberate practice that focuses on mistakes (more about this in the next several chapters). Mistakes in learning are valuable features of the process. They induce doubt; doubt initiates search. It is a bricolage process moving from the reorganization and recombination of what we think we know to improvement of that knowledge.
3. Continued generation of diverse representations is necessary to learning. Or as Einstein said, "Imagination is more important than knowledge." Without alternative and critical perspectives on current knowledge, improvements aren't possible.
4. Ultimately, we must rely on our representations to maintain a high quality of human life. To put it another way, action is the crucial critique of knowledge. Actions are the way we test the reliability of our representations. Action and its results keep us honest.

And these principles of learning have implications for teaching.

1. A selective brain cannot be instructed, it cannot be filled or molded or easily pushed around. It can be discouraged, squashed, seduced, or implored; but it cannot be shaped.
2. If you flood a selective system it will shut down. Students look and act bored because their brains aren't dealing with the content. They aren't, in current parlance, "engaged."
3. The goal of teaching is to listen, observe, and respond to what students do when challenged by a situation, a provocation or their own ambition. Instructors then can provide conditions of deliberate practice and coach them to exploit errors to improve.
4. The key tasks of teachers are to design experiences that challenge students to act, to test their representations against problems they create and work to solve. Teaching is about providing support for the hard, messy work of learning. Learning to read "my way" wasn't easy. But it was Mrs. Witherspoon who challenged me to try, and she gave me tools that helped me succeed.

Teachers tend to assume that learning is cumulative, like filling trunks and packing cases for a voyage into the great unknown. They want students to pack all the content they'll ever need. But learning is more like the ability to pack a carry-on bag for a given destination. If you take too much stuff, you won't get it under the seat in front of you. If you take the wrong stuff, you won't have what you need. Rather than trying to quickly accumulate a lot of content, students need to select relevant information and carry that forward in time.

And here's an example that makes it all clear—at least that's what it did for me. Some years ago I joined a cooking tour of Tuscany. After sweeping through the glories of Florence, we settled for a week on a tourist farm where each evening we explored Italian cooking. Our master chef was reputed to be a great teacher. I expected detailed instructions and lots of encouragement. At 5 p.m. on the first day she described the five-course meal we would cook, let us choose a dish we'd prepare with a partner, and handed us recipes. A dozen of us waited for her to conduct us through the grand rustic kitchen. But all she said was "Let's get to work."

I looked at the kitchen and thought you could park several RVs in it. Staring at the platter of chicken breasts in front of me, I panicked. I needed a knife, flour, olive oil, and a frying pan. I rushed for them yelling questions at the teacher, but everyone was yelling. We all rushed to open cabinets, ducked under tables, grabbed spatulas, and scrounged through drawers. As preparations progressed, competition increased. We scrambled for table space, cutting boards, and bowls. Knives flashed and elbows flew. Heading for the stove with a loaded skillet, I was hip-checked by a retired school superintendent. Reaching for a spatula, I was karate chopped by a professor of communication. Gradually things relaxed to a rumble of questions and helpful suggestions. Out of that chaos emerged an unforgettable five-course meal. The chicken breasts more than passed muster. Gloriously tired and nursing the last of many glasses of wine at 10 p.m., I asked the teacher, "Why didn't you tell us where everything was?"

"For years I gave kitchen tours before the first meal," she answered. "I took everyone around the kitchen pointing out where things were kept. It didn't make any difference. Once we started cooking, I was pestered with questions. 'Where is this?' 'Where is that?' No one learned anything from the tour. So, I stopped doing that and just let people find things on their own when they needed them. One evening of having to find things by yourselves and everyone learns the kitchen."

References

Armstrong, J. S. (2012). Natural learning in higher education. In N. M Seel (Ed.), *Encyclopedia of the sciences of learning*. Springer.

Atran, S. (1990). *Cognitive foundations of natural history: Toward an anthropology of science.* Cambridge University Press.

Atran, S., & Sperber, D. (1991). Learning without teaching: Its place in culture. In L.T. Landsmann (Ed.), *Culture, schooling, and psychological development.* Ablex.

Branford, J., Brown, A., & Cocking, R. (Eds.). (1999). *How people learn: Brain, mind, experience and school.* National Academies Press.

Changeux, J. P. (1995). *Conversations on mind, matter, and mathematics.* Princeton University Press.

Chomsky, N. (1966). *Syntactic structures.* Mouton.

Dehaene, S. (2009). *Reading in the brain: The science and evolution of a human invention.* Viking.

Gallistel, C. R., & King, A. P. (2009). *Memory and the computational brain: Why cognitive science will transform neuroscience.* Wiley-Blackwell.

Gatto, J. (2000). *The underground history of American education: A school teacher's intimate investigation into the problems of modern schooling.* Oxford Village Press.

Geary, D. C. (1995). Reflections of evolution and culture in children's cognition: Implications for mathematics and instruction. *American Psychologist. 50*(1), 24–37. https://doi.org/10.1037//0003-066x.50.1.24

Gopnik, A. (2003). The theory theory as an alternative to the innateness hypothesis. In L. Antony & N. Hornstein (Eds.), *Chomsky and his critics.* Basil Blackwell.

Hake, R. R. (1998). Interactive-engagement versus traditional methods: A six-thousand-students survey of mechanics test data for introductory physics courses. *American Journal of Physics, 66* (1), 64–74. https://doi.org/10.1119/1.18809

Herculano-Houzel, S. (2016). *The human advantage: A new understanding of how our brain became remarkable.* MIT Press.

Lancy, D. (2010). Learning from nobody: The limited role of teaching in folk models of children's development. *An International Journal, 3,* 79–106.

Liebenberg, L. (1990). *A field guide to animal tracks of Southern Africa.* D. Philip.

Liebenberg, L. (2013). *The origin of science.* Cybertracker.

Mazur, A. (2009, January 2). Farewell, lecture? *Science, 323,* 50–51. https://mazur.harvard.edu/files/mazur/files/rep_635.pdf

Minsky, M. (2006). *The emotion machine: Common sense thinking, artificial intelligence, and the future of the human mind.* Simon & Schuster.

Piatelli-Palmarini, M. (1989). Evolution, selection and cognition: From "learning" to parameter setting in biology and the study of language. *Cognition, 31*(1), 1–44.

Sousa, D. A. (2006). *How the brain learns.* Corwin Press.

Thelen, E., & Smith, L. (1994). *Dynamic systems approach to the development of cognition and action.* MIT Press/Bradford Books.

Tolman, E. C. (1966). *Behavior and the psychological man.* University of California Press.

Young, J. Z. (1960). *Doubt and certainty in science: A biologist's reflections on the brain.* Oxford University Press.

Young, J. Z. (1979, November). Learning as a process of selection and amplification. *Journal of the Royal Society of Medicine, 72,* 801–814. https://journals.sagepub.com/doi/pdf/10.1177/014107687907201103

8

RETHINKING FAILURE AND IGNORANCE

Up to this point, I've mentioned how *failure*, the inability of a representation to produce the desired result, jumpstarts the learning processes. When we can't explain something, don't understand an outcome, or cannot successfully complete an action that motivates us to ask why, we look at other possibilities. Failure is the sharp stick that gets us moving, but our preference is for carrots. In this chapter I want to explore the power of failure and motivate us to change the negative attitudes we have about it.

Here are the questions I hear you asking: Isn't failure—the wrong answer, the blank stare, or the solution that doesn't work—the bane of learning? Aren't there students in every course afraid that they're going to fail? And aren't there lots of faculty who worry that if at least some students aren't failing in the course, then it must be a course without rigor, substance, and intellectual challenge? From these perspectives, learning means being right, having the answer, even if having the right answer provides quick but fading satisfaction and minimal learning.

In the preceding chapters I've explained that humans create abstract schemas, representations of the world that guide their choices and actions. We're born with brains predisposed to expect things to appear, be seen, be handled, or be avoided. Our genetic heritage provides basic rules about objects in motion, other minds, and language, as well as rudimentary theories of physics, biology, and social organizations. Being abstract and general, those rules and theories are limited, often in ways we don't expect and can't understand.

Our intuitions about the world fail because they don't deal with all of the details. Our mental models attend to some details and not to others, and so they fail or erroneously explain what's happening in the world outside us.

But we can improve our models if we learn from failure. As children we find this easy and fun. Mistakes make us come up with new models that work better which in turn gives us an almost fatal even tragic confidence in our knowledge. The more we think we know, the less we want to be wrong.

Accepting Ignorance—It Can Lead Us to Learning

We don't think much about our ignorance or even our reliance on numerous other brains living or dead. Our own personal brains are so complex and made up of so many specialized modules that we are seldom aware that consciousness is but a raft floating on seas of ignorance. Nowhere is that ignorance more important but more denied than in the classroom. The paradigm of fact-based content stifles awareness of what we don't know about the world. Professors transfer information naked of all except the most obvious unknowns. Knowledge is packaged in lectures that instill the illusion of coverage. Students then organize, note, and memorize without questioning.

The relationship between knowledge and ignorance has been described by the mathematician Blaise Pascal. He envisioned that we exist in bubbles of knowledge—within the bubble is what we know and outside it what we don't know. In this view humans are wise to the extent that they are aware of the limits of their minds. As the bubble of knowledge grows, its surface contact with the unknown enlarges geometrically and becomes what is called the *proximate zone of ignorance*. Paradoxically, it expands more rapidly than our knowledge. The more we know the more we encounter ignorance. Knowledge is a kind of learned ignorance. Knowledge does not create ignorance, but it does cause collisions with it.

Take a recipe for beef bourguignon. It provides a model for producing a classic French burgundy stew. The recipe or model assumes that the cook knows the details of the kitchen, pans, appliances, utensils, and what the recipe means by pork belly, lardons, round, rump, and flanken. The recipe may be detailed, recommending what to buy, how to chop, seasonings to add, and the expected cooking time, but it is the worm's eye view of the minutiae involved in making that grand stew. Inexperienced cooks must recognize (but they usually don't) that much of the recipe they don't understand. Their current representation of cooking is ignorant of many essential details. Because the inadequate models in the aspiring cook's head are unavailable to the recipe author, the recipe is based on some wrong assumptions and therefore fails to produce a first-rate stew. To produce a dish that reaches the heights of a Julia Child bourguignon requires many hours of practice, much failure, and learning.

But talking about our ignorance—all that we don't know—is unpleasant. No one wants to be ignorant and when we find out that we are, we're dismayed. We manage by trying to avoid it and focus on our success. Since 1984, the surgeon, Marlys Witte has run a Summer Institute on Medical Ignorance at the University of Arizona to introduce students and researchers to a new field she calls *ignoramics*—the art and science of recognizing and dealing with ignorance. The fundamental assumption of ignoramics is that the world we inhabit is too complex for any person or group to know. The goal is to make people comfortable with talk about both failure and ignorance. It offers an alternative to the pursuit of innovation by mining previous knowledge—*informatics* is the storage and classification of knowledge. Informatics assumes that all the answers to the burning problems of medical research can be found in what we already know. Witte teaches that the search for better ways to organize and access knowledge is important, but not as important as learning from ignorance (Witte et al., 1989).

Medical history shows that innovative treatments—the big breakthroughs—result from wrestling with ignorance. Witte notes that medical curricula seldom address the issue that new cures have to be invented, that is, imagined, remade from what we know, but in radically astonishing ways. Access to that future lies in the failures of today; the cracks and crevices that allow escape from our cognitive bubbles. Pascal (1965) would remind us that our enormous knowledge base gives us more opportunities to connect with fertile ignorance. When we apply knowledge, the tinkering adjustments, the kludges and the workarounds reveal our ignorance and that inspires learning.

Stuart Firestein, a professor of neuroscience at Columbia University who specializes in the olfactory brain systems (smells and stinks), has written two small but powerful books, *Failure: Why Science is so Successful* (2016a) and *Ignorance: How It Drives Science* (2016b).

In his undergraduate course, which surveys the current state of ignorance in the world of science, Firestein teaches that science produces ignorance, which in turn fuels more science. The better the science, the more important is the ignorance that drives it. Scientific success depends on developing a comfort with ignorance, a willingness to be beguiled by it. Lay persons can best understand science by focusing on the ignorance instead of the landfills of fact (2016b). In other words ignore the answers and work on the questions. What we know is never safe from challenges and revisions.

If ignorance is what we don't know, and what we don't know that we don't know, how do we confront it? Accepting that the realm of ignorance is in the future helps us understand the arguments of scientists like Firestein and Witte (and others) that successful research depends on "ignorance management." If we only ask questions that we can't answer or that are beyond the time and funds available, that won't do us much good. The goal is to push against the boundaries of our current knowledge (inside the wall of Pascal's bubble, our proximate zone of ignorance) through the use of our imagination.

We get stuck when we are mesmerized by what we know. Compiling does not substitute for creativity. We need to focus our curiosity on what is possible. What is missing is often under our noses. Failures shout that something is wrong with our assumptions and the models that drive our routines. If we pay attention to failures, explore and think about them, they can inspire us to rethink our long-held beliefs. That is the way science works, Firestein maintains; it progresses from failure to failure which leads to dramatic changes in the way we think about possibilities. All systems of belief claim to be right and accumulate information, stories and data to back that claim. The difference with the scientific thought system is that it tentatively accepts only those claims that have the potential to be wrong. "Science is trustworthy because it can fail" (2016a, p. 171). In that spirit the ways we think about teaching and learning need to be scientific.

In sum, ignorance is essential to learning. If we are to learn, we can't avoid or be embarrassed by what we don't know. When we use what we know, or think we know, and it fails, what we don't know leads us to questions that inspire the search for answers and thereby expands our knowledge. The failed mental model of how we learn must be revised and improved. We can start by changing how we think about ignorance and then move on to changing our views of failure.

Learning From Failure: Necessary but Not Easy

Failure is endemic to life. The history of evolution is a spectacular record of failure—all species become extinct. Every year in the United States, 10% of businesses collapse under the garrote of competition. Touted policies, programs, and wars seldom meet expectations. The best athletic programs falter. In the academic world students and scholars fail. But higher education tries to relabel all poor results, no matter how meager or how faulty, as signs of vigor that predict a world-class future. Beneath this rhetoric lies a darker world of faculty discontent, less student effort, unchanged teaching methods, and a desperate struggle for resources. Failure is a fact of educational life. Why do educators try to disguise and deny it?

Amy Edmondson (2011) points out that learning from failure is not simple or easy. She notes that we all learn at some point that to admit failure means you take the blame. As long as instructors and students assume the connection between failure and blame, we toil in fear. If only we could discuss failures without blame. But to some that means a loss of accountability. They reason that if students explore failures instead of avoid them, classrooms would be chaos. Where is the discipline? Without blame how do we grade? Without blame, what would motivate students? Edmondson argues that the coupling of failure and blame results because we don't notice that there are different kinds of failure. Some failures result from sabotage, some from negligence, and some from lack of ability. But others result from system complexity and uncertainty. And still others from experimentation with different ways to do things. Failures are preventable, inevitable, or intelligent.

Engineers' define failure as "the space between the performance we expect and the performance that we get" (Carper, 1996, p. 57). Henry Petroski (2006) persuasively argues that dissatisfaction with what is, in light of what we want, not necessity, is the mother of invention.

We tend to think of the corporate world as one of conformity and success, but this view comes from press releases and stockholder meetings that accentuate the positive. Corporations operate in worlds where revolutions, fads, and even silliness can wipe out plans and products. Global volatile markets demand flexible organizations. Consult the biographies of corporate heroes—Ford, Hershey, Yerkes, or Carnegie—and you find tales of failure. Corporations seldom live longer than 30 years. Firms go bankrupt, get bought out, or merge. Managers must be concerned with innovations as well as efficient routines. Among entrepreneurs, failure is a badge of courage.

The management world wrestles more openly with failure than does the academic world. Universities seem never to fail. Academic programs are all trombones and banners. Failure is a word unspoken in its cloistered halls. A failed academy is a scandal. It is as if universities and schools exist in a world that seldom changes or challenges. Tomorrow always looks like today only better. Like the Whig theory of history, education progresses by building on past success, failures being the nasty flies that buzz and annoy while we consecrate knowledge beyond the vagaries of human experience.

Sim Sitkin (1992), Duke University professor of management, notes that failure is essential to learning—but it is also taboo. While success promotes stable short-term performance it also encourages over confidence in old routines, restricts attention, and limits experimentation. Success ratifies the status quo and averts risk. Failure subverts the usual and promotes risk-taking. The more uniform the practices and extreme the success, the more monolithic the organization's culture, according to Sitkin.

Learning under these conditions consists in finding successful solutions to scaled-down problems which ensures success, albeit small wins. Positive feedback fosters faster but suboptimal performance. In contrast, failure focuses attention on ignored problems, inconsistencies, fuzzy explanations, and ambiguous results. Further, failure stimulates action by providing exacting goals—the things that need to be fixed that tend to unfreeze old habits of seeing, talking, and thinking.

Experience with modest failures—"small flops"—promotes risk-taking, experimentation, and resilience. The more intelligent the failures, the more information produced. The increased range of responses promotes a greater variety of ideas and perspectives in the organization. Under these conditions learning can be slow as more options are considered. People can openly recognize and discuss failure, and routinely challenge assumptions. Such a culture provides opportunities for innovation.

I've used medicine and business to showcase the positive role failure can play in advancing knowledge. Accepting a failure, taking away notions of blame, drives us toward innovation. When an action fails, it's there to be learned from, if we can accept it. But when I tried to change students' thinking about failures and mistakes, I discovered firsthand that, as necessary as it is, that doesn't mean it's easy.

The Problem With Correcting Mistakes

Any new model of learning must address the way that mistakes allow us to improve knowledge, and I discovered how difficult is to address student mistakes constructively. Upon finding a student mistake or confusion, my first reaction was dismay which I followed with attempts to eliminate the mistakes. In the beginning, I thought it was my teaching that was causing their failures and I made great efforts to improve my teaching. Yet all of those efforts were hampered by attempts to reduce my mistakes. That was until I started to realize that the way I improved was to experiment, to fail, to modify, and to fail again—all the time gradually changing my representations or understanding of how students learned. I didn't end up a perfect teacher, but when I changed my thinking about failure and started implementing the very process I wanted the students to follow, I started learning about teaching.

But my students continued to experience their mistakes as a source of great distress. The more opportunities I provided for students to learn by doing, the more mistakes they made. When I could get them to discuss the causes and the ways to recover, their mistakes became "teachable moments." My worst failures came when I enthusiastically revealed students' failures. Early on, I'd identify every mistake a student made in an assignment. Some reacted fearfully and seemed to redouble their efforts. Some just dropped the class. One brave student brought her graded essay to my office, placed it on my desk and said, "You've ruined it!"

Her eyes burned through tears. The tension in her hands showed the effort it was taking to rein in her anger. I immediately consoled, "You wrote the best essay on Plato's *Republic* in the class . . . "

"So why did you write these nasty comments?"

"They're not nasty. I was just trying to help by pointing out the things you could improve."

She flipped to a page of the essay and shoved it toward me. "Look at this page. You scribbled all over it." And she began to read: "obscure, this doesn't follow, straw man, where is the conclusion? Awk! And what does that mean A-W-K? Look you wrote it here and here and here," she flipped through the pages.

"It means awkward. Your sentences are long and convoluted. That makes it hard for the reader to understand."

"You don't think this graffiti makes it hard for me to understand what you want?

"It isn't about what I want. It's about helping you develop your talents as a writer and thinker. I think you're gifted."

"I think that's crap," she hurled at me, tore out of the office and never came back to class.

One of the most intelligent, motivated, and literate students I had met and she was gone. That was a big mistake; one that I couldn't correct and still mourn.

But it was a failure I learned from. I backed off from pointing out every mistake and focused on ones that were most troublesome or that revealed problems with implications elsewhere in the paper. Even so, mistakes were bad events; they hurt and confused students.

So I tried simplifying the assignments, hoping to head off mistakes, but that blocked learning. For example, I assigned op-ed pieces for criticism. Often extraneous material made it more difficult to determine the author's purpose. Did she want to anticipate an outcome, cause or block something from happening, or choose one action over another? To reduce errors, I edited and simplified. The result, of course, was to botch the learning. Real authors in the world present their arguments to persuade not enable criticism. Students could master my toy assignments without learning how to criticize actual efforts. They got better at the practice but not better at the skill of criticizing real policy recommendations.

I was caught in a paradox of my own making. If the students acted, they made mistakes. Those mistakes upset me and them, and that made them try harder to not make errors. I tried to reduce the challenge of the assignments to make mistakes less frequent. Both our impulses stifled learning—less initiative, fewer challenges, fewer opportunities for them to find ways to improve. The seemingly obvious way out—to accept the mistakes and strive to find ways to recover—eluded me at first although I opportunistically began to move in that direction. To reduce student anxiety, I began to talk about the necessity of failures in learning something new. They weren't having it. I labeled assignments "Fast Failure Exercises," distributed M&Ms to reward mistakes, and called the most audacious and inventive errors "creative mistakes." The students made me change the label to "Fast Learning" and ate the candy.

Why Teachers Need to Fail Better

Firestein (2016a) calls upon us to "fail better." Really? That is not easy. Even when we recognize that we can learn from failure, the idea is to get the failure over so we can succeed. So why would we want to go through the trouble of failing better, even failing spectacularly?

The idea of "failing better" comes from Samuel Beckett, the Nobel Laurate novelist and playwright. He was one of those remarkable artists who never reprised himself. He refused throughout his career to do what had made him famous. Failure for Beckett was a strategy to avoid repeating the obvious. He wanted to look beyond what he knew which required him to "fail better," that is to question, to doubt, to exult in uncertainty. Firestein thinks that should be a model for scientists. I think it should be a model for teachers.

Where there is learning, there are failures. Much of what effective teachers do is to create situations in which students apply what they know and then fail. That makes it possible for them to see the need to change and improve their representations, those explanatory models they use to make sense of things. Since only they can change those schemas, these intrusive challenges are fundamental to teaching.

If teachers can't learn from their failures in the classroom, then it isn't likely that their students will either. Unless our students see us make, recognize, and correct our mistakes, we can't expect them to grasp that mistakes are a key to learning. Failures have interesting, if humbling, things to say about our long-held and unnoticed assumptions about learning. Just as failures help students understand their ignorance, they can free teachers from persistent but unexamined mental manacles that plague the profession.

Perhaps the first barrier is the embarrassing fact that we fail most of the time. Take almost any standard teaching practice: questioning, discussion, lectures, grading assignments, critiquing student performances, 50-minute classes, assigning textbooks, fixation on motivation, repeated exposition, undifferentiated feedback, emphasis on information transfer—you name it. In every case, there is research evidence that such practices work, but only some of the time and for some of the students. Mostly their effects are mediocre.

Years of research, some of it explored in chapter 4 on questioning, indicate that teacher questions do not promote student thinking and lectures don't either (see chapter 3). The feedback provided on graded assignments may be read but is regularly ignored. Most techniques for motivating students fail badly. Teacher attempts to transfer large amounts of information result in rote memorization and short retention. Ignoring the time it takes for students to learn has resulted in curricula crammed with too much content. Yet these failures go unexplored. They are not evidence of our incompetence. They are signs of our ignorance and our great potential to improve. Only when we ignore them in a rush for success do they do damage.

Nothing blinds us like a long-accepted assumption. Our belief that students learn best when they are being instructed by teachers explains away our failures and inures us to the shortcomings of our assumptions. We end up with only a vague sense that there's something wrong with what we do in the classroom.

Instead of instructing by repeating what we already know, we could be creating learning environments in which students learn from their mistakes and teachers can learn from theirs. In these environments, students would be free to demonstrate their knowledge. A teacher wouldn't jump in to judge and rob students of opportunities to see errors and ways to correct them. A teacher could respond to student efforts and support their trials, giving the kind of actionable feedback that promotes learning. And by failing better—using our imagination and passion to innovate—we could make teaching the exciting enterprise in practice we'd love it to be.

It was understanding the need and value of confronting failure that caused me to make my courses failure-focused. I did so with the goal of encouraging students to recognize and explore mistakes from which they could learn. But something else happened as well. Focusing on failure changed the way I dealt with it, as a person and as a teacher. As I tried and failed to sell this perspective to students, I searched for alternatives. I discovered some that first helped me learn from my failures and then helped students deal with theirs. But besides learning to deal with ignorance and failure, we also had to learn to deal with criticism.

References

Carper, K. L. (1996). Construction pathology in the United States. *Structural Engineering International, 6*(1), 57–60. https://doi.org/10.2749/101686696780496085

Edmondson, A. C. (2011, April). Strategies for learning from failure. *Harvard Business Review, 89*(4), 48–55. https://hbr.org/2011/04/strategies-for-learning-from-failure

Firestein, S. (2016a). *Failure: Why science is so successful.* Wiley-Blackwell.

Firestein. S. (2016b). *Ignorance: How it drives science.* Wiley-Blackwell.

Pascal, B. (1965). *Selections from the thoughts of Pascal.* Wiley-Blackwell.

Petroski, H. (2006). *Success through failure: The paradox of design.* Princeton University Press.

Sitkin, S. (1992). Learning through failure: The strategy of small losses in L. L. Cummings & B. Shaw (Eds.), *Research in organizational behavior.* JAI Press.

Witte, M., Kerwin, A., Witte, C. L., & Scadron, A. (1989). A curriculum on medical ignorance. *Medical Education 23*(1), 24–29. https://doi.org/10.1111/j.1365-2923.1989.tb00808.x

9

CRITICISM

The Key to Learning

In my senior year we were assigned Shakespeare, the greatest English author, father of our mother tongue, and I declared war. We not only had to read, we had to appreciate him. If *The Merchant of Venice* left us dumbfounded, we were unworthy. I resisted, refusing to go along with what I was supposed to believe. Searching for authors who criticized Shakespeare, I happened onto the immense nutty literature debunking Shakespeare's authorship and it seduced me. I espoused various conspiracies in class, proposing that perhaps the author was a better educated scholar like Bacon, a worldly aristocrat like Edward de Vere, or the playwright, Kit Marlowe. My rants darkened the teacher's face.

To better flummox and flex my polemical skills I read more, and that included more of Shakespeare's plays. Even as I resisted "bardolatry" I learned something of how to read the bard, but that failed to convince me of his greatness. Shakespeare was a popularizer, a borrower, a money grubber, and a toady to the rich; overrated compared to great authors like Edgar Allen Poe and Mark Twain. By the time I'd finished making these points, I'd expended more effort than anyone in the class. I wrote a culminating essay proving beyond a doubt that Francis Bacon wrote the plays. I got a B- in the course.

A year later I was a freshman in an English course on literary criticism, a topic I deemed uninteresting and irrelevant. We were assigned to read *Richard II*. With help from a dictionary, I struggled through it. A debonair, tweedy, and smart professor was my new opponent.

"What's the meaning of that speech, Spence?" he asked.

I fumbled, "It's to please the groundlings." My classmates booed. "Shakespeare was clever and had to fill the theater to survive," I rushed on. "The play was about overthrowing a king; that could be treason. He had to sound like a patriot."

The professor smiled at me. "Now that is not the best way to criticize an author," he began. "Shakespeare did face problems of money and political censorship. But it is how he solved those problems within the structure and language of the play that interests us. Notice the particular character of these words, 'other Eden' and 'demi-paradise' instead of 'Eden' or 'paradise.' What do you think, Spence?"

A fog lifted, "He is comparing the fall of Richard with the fall of man."

"Yes, and how does he do that?"

The discussion ran on, conducted so that the powerful principles of criticism were revealed: Stick to the text, read closely, analyze the metaphors, seek out the paradoxes, and mark how the author manipulates literary devices to create tension. I returned to my room to read the play again, now questioning every line. I fell in love with this subtle but intense way to read and quickly became a Shakespeare fanatic. And that was how I learned the value of criticism. What I came to understand subsequently was that its value extends beyond the literary criticism I used to tackle Shakespeare. In fact, criticism is key to learning, but not a key that easily unlocks the doors to understanding.

It turns out that criticism is the portal to that zone of proximate ignorance where what we know bumps up against what we don't know. Criticism opens that door to new knowledge at two different junctures. We start with what we already know, we make mistakes. But the mistakes can be the chinks and handholds that help us escape from our cognitive jails. They enable us to find the way out—why did it happen, what assumptions apparently aren't true, is what we thought only partly wrong or totally wrong? With that initial critique of our understanding, we start the search for alternatives, other ideas, theories, and possible explanations. At that point criticism gives us a way to winnow our conjectures and focus on those worth trying out.

Critical Thinking: Hard to Accept, Difficult to Learn

But using criticism isn't simple or easy. Consider the efforts that the National Transportation Safety Board puts into every aircraft failure and the resulting improvements in airline safety (see Syed, 2015). We make criticism difficult with our confused and conflicted feelings about it. We distinguish between constructive and destructive criticism, which often means dismissing criticisms that we don't like. It seems that criticism and failure are simultaneously bad and good. We avoid and revel in them. We want to learn quickly so we can quit failing. Conversely, we aspire to become critical thinkers so that we can challenge our own thinking and that of others.

Like a receding tide, criticism reveals intellectual detritus and naked experts. We assume that most people aren't very good at it. Left to themselves people confirm their own opinions, reject counter ideas, and value their own self-righteousness over logic and evidence. Most people evaluate truth claims with a "makes sense" epistemology—true statements just sound right and make sense. Like ballet, critical thinking seems unnatural and learning it, a strenuous failure for most who try.

Critical thinking undermines our confidence in the stories we believe about ourselves and the world. We exaggerate and reify those beliefs to deny our ignorance. Like water bugs we skitter on the surface of reality and ignore the turbulence and menace that lurks below. When faced with difficult questions we substitute less rigorous ones. Usually we learn things the easiest way we can and live with mediocre results. Thus, our cognitive life is shadowed, menaced by illusions, and strangled by arrogance.

Criticism makes learning a perilous experience, emotionally and intellectually. We don't itch to reform our representations—despite the value of doing so. But we live in a dangerously uncertain world. Educators suggest, and rightly, that to thrive in such a world, our citizens need to be scientifically literate, numerate, and critical. Unfortunately, in the opinion of many, higher education is not producing enough informed citizens to manage and improve our condition. To graduate students able to critically think we must stop making education about transmitting the wisdom of the past and use it instead to locate the gaps, exaggerations, and mistakes of that wisdom; either educational is critical or it's a waste of time.

Critical Thinking: Challenging to Teach

It didn't take long in my teaching career to discover that students lacked the critical reasoning abilities they needed to participate in the classroom activities I wanted to pursue. It's impossible to teach a subject like political theory if students can't confront and argue with ideas. I wanted students to have the skills and confidence to interpret, argue with, understand the limits of, and mentally experiment with the solutions proposed by past thinkers. I wanted to coach thinkers who could improvise.

I, like most teachers, wasn't sure how to teach critical thinking and we don't have a good track record of successfully doing it. In 1984 *A Nation at Risk* (National Commission on Excellence in Education) famously declared that nearly 40% of high school seniors could not make valid inferences from a body of written findings. Since then, programs designed to develop critical thinking skills have proliferated, but so far there hasn't been much sign of improvement. Assessments of prominent programs show mixed results at best. We all agree that students should learn to think critically, but classroom practices deny its importance (Browne & Meuti, 1999).

Scholars in higher education resist the idea that critical thinking is a set of generic skills that can be taught independent of subject matter. They claim that it's central to the learning of any subject and uniquely shaped by the nature of the subject matter. The distinction often made between active and passive learning highlights the difference between thinking while learning, versus learning without thinking at all.

What made critical thinking difficult for me to teach involved the emotional reactions of students to failure. I witnessed the responses to failure I explored in the previous chapter. To have an idea criticized, by ourselves or by others, puts the idea to test, not the recipient of the critique. It was the idea that didn't work, but that's a hard concept for students to accept. They take failure personally when in fact, the idea didn't work because there are better ideas and solutions that make more sense. It's criticism that offers a way to identify them. Deep, lasting learning involves criticism, and criticism only works if we accept failure as an inherent part of learning. If critical reasoning is possible (and it is), can be improved through practice (and it can), and that is what has enabled the survival of our species, then it should be a major component of education. What we need are successful ways to teach it.

The Creation of a New Tool for Criticism

A political scientist, Eugene J. Meehan (1988), believed that the enterprise of science changed drastically in the early 20th century. He proposed that the new science of Einstein and quantum mechanics involved a changed role for human investigators. The old billiard-ball world existed absent of human purpose or imagination. It was as cold, simple, and star-sprinkled as a night sky. The new world of curved space-time and quantum mechanics was intractably complex, so much so that the human mind could only speculate about how it worked. Scientists who once watched the laws of nature drive cosmic mechanisms now found themselves within a swirling world where reality had to be fathomed by means of theories. Nature turned out to be wilder than our soaring fictions. Human representations resulted in understandings of the world that were limited by sensory and neuronal capacities. There could be no grand theory of everything, only theories of specific situations relevant to human survival.

Quantum mechanics—a theory of the way things work at the subatomic level—illustrates this new volatile understanding of nature. Quantum mechanics implies that what we see around us is not the world as it is. Furthermore, the world does not work the way we think it does. As Adrian Kent (2014), a quantum philosopher, notes "Quantum theory might not be fundamentally correct, but it would not have worked so well for so long if its strange and beautiful mathematics did not form an important part of the deep structure of nature" (para. 50). This new way of understanding nature destroyed the deterministic universe and replaced it with a new interpretation of a reality where we can't expect certainties. The success of physicists in overthrowing their own flawed theories of the universe is an exemplar of successful criticism powered by critical thinking.

From Meehan's (1967) perspective science is a form of inquiry into the ways we organize and explain our experience. It depends on human ingenuity and judgment to create theories or useful guesses about how humans can thrive. He writes:

> Science, in brief, has become a distinctly human enterprise. Its needs and accomplishments can only be measured relative to man; its modes of inquiry are determined by human interests and the limits of human capacity. Science is simply what man can do for man, using experience as a guide. (p. 55)

He insisted that the selection of an epistemology is a navigational change, not the plotting of a detailed itinerary before undertaking a voyage (Meehan, 1965). What we already know, as imperfect as it is, informs and constrains our knowledge. We try to improve knowledge but not reinvent it. With a bootstrap approach like this, social scientists could promote piecemeal and corrigible social knowledge. That would let us do our best to understand society, psychology, and learning without arbitrary and universal formulas on how we do it. We begin by opening conventions, habits, traditions, laws, institutions, constitutions, decisions, and history to criticism and the critical thinking needed to change them.

After Popper's (1976) conjectures that knowledge has no foundations and yet serves well human purposes, Meehan's is a practical next step in the reform of inquiry. He plundered the philosophical controversies ignited by the revolution in scientific thought to liberate the social sciences from outdated creeds. He was not so much a big thinker as an artisan focused on creating tools of criticism. I think of his theory of knowledge as more of a theory of application—the representation of an engineer, not a philosopher.

After his early years of critiquing the intellectual assumptions of social science inquiry, Meehan created a simplified model of knowledge application. Rather than slog through dicey philosophical disputes, he proposed a method to improve public policies. That was the great appeal of his work for me. A policy in this view is an action rule that applies a priority to force a decision in a given situation. What a policy accomplishes can then be used to criticize the underlying knowledge assumptions.

Proposed actions themselves cannot be meaningfully criticized before they are implemented but we can criticize the assumptions and reasoning which underlies them. We can learn vicariously, eliminating our poorest ideas before the expense of public trials. We can also learn from policy failures, actions that do not garner the desired results. We can exploit those failures to refine and repair our theories of the social and political world. Meehan's project was a system for evaluating knowledge claims that could be used to bolster or criticize public policies and a way to improve conceptions of research. This allows us to undertake the reasonable goal of improving human knowledge and avoid the tyrannical and often murderous goal of improving human beings. And this approach can also be a way to teach students critical thinking. But first we must move from what Meehan proposed theoretically to how it works pragmatically.

Meehan's Theory of Knowledge Offers a Criteria for Critical Thinking

Theories can link human actions to the achievement of a purpose. That purpose can be simple, like maintaining body temperature, or complicated, like constructing a bridge. Each case requires subpurposes such as obtaining a warm coat or producing girders of a proper strength. In the simpler cases we rely on habits and rules of thumb. In complex cases we rely on elaborate plans that radiate out from the primary purpose to form chains of interlocking activities.

Meehan proposed a theory of knowledge restricted to a few general patterns that can be used to make decisions that can then be implemented. His theory sweeps away a lot of controversy and leaves a set of relatively simple instruments that could be used and mastered. These patterns and instruments represent a version of critical thinking. The brevity and power of the model cuts through the philosophical fog and operates in the intellectual world much like the microworld of the tee-ball apparatus in baseball. It allows a practice space where critical skills can be safely tried. His framework does not guarantee better results no matter what, but it does provide critical tools for revision and refinement.

Here's an example of how Meehan's framework can be used to help us. As educated consumers, we are beset with essays, op-ed pieces, academic journal articles, editorials, blogs, rants, and other forms of expression that attempt to suggest or tell us what to think and do. Their quality ranges from brilliant to baloney. Our job is to figure out whether any of those written materials can help us improve how we understand the world. Here's how Meehan proposes we make that decision.

Step 1: *What is the author's purpose?* What we want to establish in critiquing a piece is what we will call the author's analytical purpose. Specifically, we need to decide if he or she wants to persuade us about what will happen, how to make or stop something from happening, or what to choose to happen. Note: Authors sometimes disguise or are confused about their purposes; that makes their claims immune from criticism.

Step 2: *Will the author's purpose improve the quality of life of a human population?* If not, the article falls outside the knowledge theory.

Step 3: *Which type of purpose is the author trying to fulfill?* There are three types of purposes that employ knowledge to inform our actions: anticipate—anticipate what will happen in the future; control—make or stop something from happening; choose—select the best action from available options.

Step 4: *Given an author's purpose what has to be done to achieve it?* Each type of purpose requires one or more generalized patterns to meet its goal. To anticipate requires concepts, classifications, or forecasts; to control requires a causal theory; and to choose requires theories, normative variables, preferences, and policies.

Once we find the patterns in the article, we can determine (a) whether they are appropriate given the purpose; (b) whether they are well formulated—concepts defined, rules clear-cut, limiting conditions specified; (c) whether they are supported by evidence or argument; and (d) whether the problem situation fits the patterns. If an article fails any of these tests—doesn't have a significant purpose, appropriate patterns, well-constructed and supported patterns—its claim to knowledge must be rejected pending further work.

Mathew Lipman (1988) suggested that the word "criterial" should be seen as a synonym for "critical"—to think critically is to think in light of using criteria. It is not enough to encourage generic criticism. Everyone can run, but to run competitively or even jog without injury requires specific skills developed through a special kind of practice (much more about this in the chapter on deliberative practice). Repetition won't do. It is all too easy to repeat faults.

All of this makes criticism an intellectual skill—critical thinking. Students and teachers can criticize; what they both need is a structure—a representation that allows them to use criteria to deliberately practice criticism. Meehan contributed a model, a language, and criteria that could be used to teach critical reasoning, and that's what I'd been looking for. The model's attraction was the quality of practice it made possible.

Meehan believed that we used a knowledge process something like this unconsciously every day, but rarely, in times of trouble, or in novel situations are we pressed to do it consciously and reflectively. Only then do we confront the need to choose an epistemology and use representations of the social world. But the big game is how we do this in the public sphere where policies can determine the fate of organizations, communities, and states. There Meehan's model of the thinking process can enable citizens, experts, and officials to criticize, deliberate, and test ideas. Social, political, and economic entities might then learn from their mistakes. That would not result in a perfect world, but it might be a better one. Meehan's response to the need to train aid workers in overseas development illustrates that kind of improvement.

Well-educated technicians from more developed economies and polities did poorly in their efforts to assist developing communities to control and improve their environments. For example, villages in tropical climates needed to reduce their exposure to malaria by changing the way sewage and storm water flow were managed. It turned out to be harder than expected. Technical solutions that worked in donor countries failed in local conditions. Highly efficient pumps provided to improve water supply sat idle because no one understood how they worked or should be maintained. The technologies needed to be adapted to local conditions. That took a teaching program, and Meehan's (1994) coaching model turned out to be a useful teaching tool—a way to describe and explain what was being taught that allowed instructors, students, and clients to assess (test what they'd learned) by looking at performance (p. 176). He demonstrated that aid workers could be quickly trained to teach using this representation of knowledge.

Shortly after discovering Meehan's work, I was asked to teach a graduate methods course. My department colleagues were not satisfied with graduate students' research and writing performances. The course description said that students would learn "how to think scientifically and produce practical research designs." There was my goal: Improve graduate students' ability to undertake, organize, and complete independent research. There was the assessment: colleagues who were satisfied with the students' performance. That combination of goal and assessment sounded like it had potential. I decided to try it.

Does Meehan's Approach to Critical Thinking Work in a Classroom?

Fresh from my own thesis research on the epistemological foundation of political knowledge, I was determined to liberate these future political scientists from the thrall of obsolete theories of knowledge. We would read and discuss criticisms of empiricism, paradoxes of the so-called scientific method science and the limits of logic as a research guide. The course motto was Paul Feyerabend's (1993) declaration: "What is needed is the development of a methodology which allows for, and perhaps even demands the use of our imagination."

We read philosophers of science such as Popper, Mach, Quine, Frege, Duhem, Kuhn, Hemple, Hanson, and Lakatos. The course was great entertainment (the graduate students happily discussed these philosophers of science), but it ended up being awful preparation for professional research. Final papers revealed that students could mimic the discourse of the Vienna Circle but could not competently criticize a knowledge claim, analyze an argument, or interpret a data set. A few months later when I interviewed the students on their research progress, I knew the course had failed. Most students told me that they just needed to find a way to make their data look good with minimal effort. My colleagues were not impressed. Now what? My idea was worse than wrong, and I was assigned to teach the course again.

I decided to use Meehan's (1971) *The Foundations of Political Analysis: Empirical and Normative* as a text for my next try. Since his patterns seemed easy to describe and illustrate, I plunged into teaching a coaching language I barely understood. When I introduced the vocabulary, students quickly objected; they resisted new definitions for old terms like knowledge, information, and theory. As recent graduates they assumed they knew political science basics and now wanted to undertake professional tasks. They had learned habits of drive-by criticism; show what an author didn't do; what articles she didn't cite, or what ideas he ignored. They insisted that was the professional way and brought examples from journals and lectures in support.

But I held an ace in the hole—they had a thesis staring at them. I countered their objections with "This will get you started. Write up a one-page description of your topic or area. What do you want to do—anticipate events or trends, control some, or choose an action? Do you want to show that some study purporting to forecast is faulty? Do you want to demonstrate the superiority of a policy?"

The first results were unequivocal. The graduate students hated the course. Years later one explained: "We thought we knew political science. You kept insisting that we do things we couldn't do. Sure we were sore, but it was the best thing you could have done. Of course, you were hard on us—sarcastic and pushy just like a coach. I don't think you yelled, but we all knew you wanted to." The course worked. Weeks and months after the course it over, even the most negative students came by my office to thank me. A repeat had the same results, research skills improved and faculty advisors were pleased, but the course was never popular.

Another opportunity came floating down the halls of ivy—a new honors program. A requirement of the program was that honors students do original research and write a thesis during their senior year. A faculty member had to advise their efforts and certify its quality. The first cohort was inept at research and writing. Those professors who signed on as thesis advisors were dismayed and wanted to end the program. Our approach was to urge students to write about their interest in a topic and then go to the library. "Tell us what you want to say, and see what information and knowledge you need to say that." That frightened them. Students collected far more information than they needed or could understand (they confirmed what's in chapter 5, mountains of information does not add up to knowledge). They mucked about without guiding questions, filling laptops and pads with notes and citations. Their sprawling papers were difficult to read and hard to critique. As a remedy I proposed an honors course called Critical Reasoning in Political Science, required in the junior year as preparatory for all students intending to complete an honors thesis. On the endorsement of several colleagues who had seen the improvement in graduate student preparation, the department accepted the proposal.

Before I continue with what happened in the honors course, I need make a point about feedback and when it is most meaningful—I write more at length on feedback in chapter 11 on its role in deliberative practice. For now, it's important to address our sense that learning is best measured in the future. When students complain, "Why am I learning this?" or want to quit, because "This is not worth the effort," we all say the same thing: "One day this knowledge will be important to you. You will use it to be successful in your work and life." Unfortunately, we say it too often and rarely try to find out if it is true.

Feedback is central to improving learning and teaching, everyone agrees. Unless we can compare what we intend with what we get, we are lost. The achievements of education are long term. The relation between grade point averages and lifetime success is weak at best. Exams, recitations, projects, essays, and problems are limited ways to measure student learning. Regurgitating a formula or writing an essay with all the right words does not predict a student's performance. That only shows that students understand the procedures and vocabularies of practice.

If a learner's representations of reality become more sophisticated, corrigible, and relevant, they should be better doctors, citizens, writers, or politicians. That is the whole point. Applying the patterns of knowledge, like using a map to explore wilderness or a recipe to cook a pot roast, indicates knowledge at a deeper level. The real test of knowledge is the ability to improvise and succeed under real-world conditions. Instructors are in the same situation. Since what students do in class poorly predicts lifetime achievement, teachers too need to measure the students' professional performances. There are few opportunities to do that. Alumni scatter and even forget their professors' names.

Stafford Beer (1979) points out that there are at least two feedback loops involved in an academic course (pp. 462–467). One involves the response of instructors to the immediate performance of students. When things go wrong—students fail assignments, don't come to class, or complain loudly—instructors can make changes in assignments, workloads, and procedures. A second loop involves instructor responses to graduate failures in their professional lives. In theory this would mean changes at the level of curriculum and course design. Beer notes that the second loop takes time and research to close. Most teacher attention is focused on the first feedback level.

Luckily, I had two independent measures of student learning in the honors course that could serve as proxies. I could use them to construct a second feedback loop. First, could students conceive and complete a professional quality research project? And second, were my colleagues who advised them satisfied with their performance on their honor theses? Those measures were independent of my assessment. That closed the loop and promised to reveal failures I could work on.

My problem was that the two loops sent me different signals. Students did not like the course. Faculty advisors did like the students' work. How could I reconcile that conflict? It seemed that Meehan's system worked and my teaching didn't. I had to sort out what I did that made learning possible and what I did that impeded it. That imperative to locate and correct my errors was a gift. It made me focus on student performance and how that related to my assignments and presentations.

Wanting to improve I took class time to deal with complaints. Students were often confused and frustrated. Meehan's text was dense and difficult to understand. They struggled with the homework. Nearly everyone said the course required too much study time and interfered with their schedules. My aggressive questioning threatened them. The in-class problem exercises were rated highly, but frustratingly difficult to work on in teams. There were never enough examples. Gradually I discovered that students indeed knew when something did not work, but seldom had ideas about solutions.

How could I redesign the course to make it more palatable? Meehan was generous with his time, experience, and advice. The more I discussed his theory of knowledge with him the more we differed on how to teach it. I tried using three of his texts and finally settled on, *The Thinking Game* (1988). He insisted that students needed to learn the theory of knowledge and then practice it on everyday problems. He reasoned that if students didn't explicitly learn the theory, they wouldn't be capable of criticizing, repairing, or improving their work. Meehan thought that students could understand his theory by reading the text before class and then having instructors lead them through discussions of it. But his own text dismissed criticism and his model of critical thinking came across as dogma. Outraged students were all too ready to critique and reject it.

Eventually I found it easier to present the theory as a system. I offered it as a way to learn critical thinking. "Try it, take for a test drive and see if it is useful. If you want to understand the background the text is online. Consult it when you are curious or stuck." I also finally figured out that these honor students were fragile. For years they had faced high expectations in school, high praise when they met expectations, and much trouble when they didn't. Anything less than an A on an assignment assaulted them and getting a C could cause crying. I explained that they could not expect an A on their first projects. They were novices that had to work out the kinks and bugs before they could expect their performances to excel. They still objected, but after completing the course students told a different story. Learning "applied epistemology" enabled them to set up and conduct independent research and excel in capstone courses or in writing their honors thesis. After they completed the course, they declared it invaluable. The more times I taught the course the more testimonials I collected. A former graduate student and successful professor, Sid Olufs, sent me this:

> I . . . had hoped that with the passage of time and 20 years of professional experience and the associated acquired wisdom that I would find *The Thinking Game* to be less challenging to read. But I am sorry to say I still find it terribly dense, hard to digest, and written with an unappealing and inaccessible academic style . . . However, I also find it more relevant than ever! And I have used the decision matrix methodology many times over the years. The two books from the undergraduate days that I still consult most often are the *Oxford Dictionary* and *The Thinking Game.*
>
> (S. Olus, personal communication)

Yes, You Can Teach Students to Think Critically

One clear blue February day, I strolled into class confident that I'd learned to teach critical thinking. I didn't look much like the young man who'd discovered criticism and learned to love Shakespeare, the eager reporter, or the young exuberant professor. My hair was thin, my paunch ample, and my eyes wrinkled at the edges. The old makeshift classroom belonged to the College of Engineering. When I badgered the registrar for a flexible room, I got a suite of chipped tables and dented chairs. The students entered knowing the drill. We hefted the long tables, arranged them in a square with chairs on both sides, and left an entrance. Now we had a practice space where the students could work in small teams and I could circulate from team to team without hazard. It wasn't pretty, but it worked.

They bent to their work. Each team was working on a problem that concerned how to anticipate future events using classifications and forecasts. The teams worked through a sequence of problems that started easy with forecasting the best time to get to the dining hall for lunch to hard ones like determining the best location for a hospital. Students called the class weird. No one looked bored and usually my worst problem was to design challenges for the faster teams. It had taken me years of iterations to get it to work. And sometimes it didn't. But today was a breeze. The class buzzed with ideas, jokes, and squabbles. As a hand went up I moved to the team to confront their quandaries.

"Creative mistake," someone shouted, "look at this. Our algorithm forecast that people will run a mile in under 10 seconds in 50 years. That can't be right but we followed all the rules and did the calculations." I launched into a minilecture on how every forecast based on extrapolations must ultimately fail because conditions change over time or, as in this case, they come up against the limits of physics and biology. I lobbed a few more examples at them, and reminded them of the explosive results of exponential trends as they returned to work.

Like a worried mosquito, my attention flew around the room, listening and watching. I looked for the drop in interest, the despairing comment, the sagging body, the glazed eyes, the change-the-topic joke, the razzing. I peeked at their notes and doodles seeking any sign that students were stuck. "This is too hard," usually means "We are missing pieces or we need a new perspective." You can't create working problems without assuming some information and knowledge of previous solutions. Those "natural as breath" assumptions can be overlooked by even the most experienced instructor. I couldn't anticipate the missing pieces that derailed learning since I was cursed by my own knowledge and the motley backgrounds of the students. So, I listened and watched for the signs—then pounced.

I grabbed a chair and sat down with the team. "Where are we?," "What's working?," or "What's not working?" As the students talked about the problem, I listened for clues. "The salesman's classification of restaurants isn't working. Have you listed reasons why that might be?" The answer comes straight from the textbook: "It could be the fault of the classification. It could be his diagnosis—the way he applies the classification."

"Which?" Now as they discuss alternatives, I want to tell them the answer. It is a terrible impulse strong and wrong. I back away. They have to work it out. When I cruise back later, they have a solution. I stop the group discussions by dinging a bell on the desk. The students explain the solution and I launch into a minilecture on all the ways a classification might fail to produce accurate expectations. Heads nod and chairs squeak telling me that attention is seeping away. But I don't feel finished and hurriedly run through the last examples.

"Back to work," I declare, and they all turn back to their tasks relieved of me. Today the students were sharp, and my remarks and stories worked. As the 75-minute class ended, the tables were dragged back to their rows, the chairs returned like soldiers facing the commanding front of the room, and the notes and diagrams erased from the boards. Still beaming, I scooped a pile of papers and books into my fat briefcase. I looked up to see him watching. He was an earnest student, not brilliant, but always getting his job done and doing his share.

"Dr. Spence, you are always talking about improving the quality of this class." I nodded. "Do you want to know how to really improve this course?" I nodded again.

"Shut up!" he said.

I grabbed my case and started for the door.

"No, you don't understand," he burst beside me as I rushed down the hall. "Those learning problems you have us work on are great. This is a terrific class"

"Then why insult me?"

"The problems are interesting—the work really gets me going. But then you stop us and start talking. Couldn't you give us more problems? Couldn't you just walk around and comment on our mistakes? When you start the big talk, I zone out. I mean, do you have to do that?"

Maybe he saw the kind of class I wanted to design; a studio, workshop, or playing field where students learned through deliberate practice; making, recognizing, and correcting mistakes. Maybe I should shut up. "Thanks for the comment," I extended my hand, "I'll think about it."

I walked back to my office, lifted by the idea that I could design assignments, watch students perform, and coach. Yes, coach—I kept coming back to it. After decades of fumbling, saving the day with personality tricks, rationalizing failures, cheering myself with bombast, or dreaming of retirement, I had a vision at the end of my trek. Teaching was not the way I supposed or wanted it to be. What I needed was precisely what I've been proposing in many chapters now, new representations—new models, new maps, and new understandings—to better detect failures, harness my imagination, and to improve my teaching.

References

Beer, S. (1979). *The heart of enterprise.* Wiley.

Browne, M. N., & Meuti, M. D. (1999, June 1). Teaching how to teach critical thinking. *College Student Journal, 33*(2), 162–170.

Feyerabend, P. (1993). *Against method* (3rd ed.). Verso.

Kent, A. (2014, January 28). What really happens in Schrodinger's box? *Aeon.* https://aeon.co/essays/what-really-happens-in-schrodinger-s-box

Lipman, M. (1988). Critical thinking: What can it be? *Educational Leadership, 45*, 38–43. https://files.ascd.org/staticfiles/ascd/pdf/journals/ed_lead/el_198809_lipman.pdf

Meehan, E. J. (1965). *The theory and method of political analysis.* Dorsey Press.

Meehan, E. J. (1967). *Contemporary political thought.* Dorsey Press.

Meehan, E. J. (1971). *The foundations of political analysis: Empirical and normative.* Dorsey Press.

Meehan, E. J. (1988). *The thinking game: A guide to effective study.* Chatham House.

Meehan, E. J. (1994). *Social inquiry: Needs, possibilities, limits.* Chatham House.

National Commission on Excellence in Education. (1984). *Nation at risk.* USA Research.

Popper, K. R. (1976). *Unended quest: An intellectual autobiography.* Fontana/Collins.

Syed, M. (2005). *Black box thinking: The surprising truth about success (and why some people never learn from their mistakes).* Penguin.

10

TEACHING THAT PROMOTES LEARNING FROM MISTAKES AND FAILURE

We are not used to teaching in ways that help students learn from mistakes and failure. My goal in this chapter is to describe three instructional approaches that support failed learning endeavors. The first one is the most important. Students can't learn from mistakes if they don't make them and they won't make mistakes unless they take action. Yes, it's active learning, but not the tricks, tips, and techniques often used to keep basically bored students engaged, it's action in the Dewey sense of learning by doing. If students are active and doing, then that raises the question, what should teachers be doing? Their principle role is that of instructional designers and I think the ideas of minimalism provide the operating principles for that role. And finally, I want to explore importance of imagination when learners turn their attention to those alternative ways of understanding and recreating their representations.

The Need for Action—It Encourages Learning

This need to take action contradicts the Platonic notion that knowledge is a product of contemplation. Unfortunately, all too often we lecture and teach like Platonists promoting contemplation by assigning readings and talking about the thoughts and actions of exemplary people whether dead or alive. In that sense our classrooms resemble Plato's cave. Students sit in the dark trying to understand the professor's shadowy abstractions. They come to believe that to learn is to witness, contemplate, absorb, and take notes. In the cave, the instructor's goal is to control the student minds, bend them to the receiving tasks and curtail their impulses to move, act, or question. But minds are slippery stuff and most students in the cave escape into daydreams or slumber.

In *Democracy and Education* Dewey (1916) argues that thinking—applying ideas and responding to the resulting insights and failures—is the basis of acquiring knowledge. He concludes that you could not transfer knowledge or impose it on students—instead, as we know from his most widely quoted statement, "students learn by doing." A generalized pattern like $E=MC^2$ could not be understood as anything more than an answer on examinations unless students can apply it and face the problems it raises. As Dewey puts it:

> No thought, no idea, can possibly be conveyed as an idea from one person to another. When it is told, it is, to the one to whom it is told, another given fact, not an idea. The communication may stimulate the other person to realize the question for himself and to think it out a like idea, or it may smother his intellectual interest and suppress his dawning effort at thought. But what he directly gets cannot be an idea. Only by wrestling with the conditions of the problem at first hand, seeking and finding his own way out, does he think. (p. 128)

Dewey's philosophy of education follows from this insight. To teach is to place students in an environment full of activities that raise problems. Students need to be interested in the activities; make observations; seek information to deal with problems; take responsibility for suggesting and developing solutions; and apply them to test their viability. And when that need to be actively involved in the processes of learning is taken away, learning is a frustrating, inconclusive experience and here's an example that will be familiar to most of us.

Learning the Computer

For many people the experience of learning computers has not been pleasant despite all of the cheerleading ads that proclaimed the excitement, ease, and joy of computer use. The early days in the 1970s and 1980s were the worst. Massive manuals, self-teaching texts, and workshops only succeeded in frustrating those who tried to master the computer.

The engineers and programmers designed the personal computers based on how they thought users would learn the computer's features and procedures. Icons like wastebaskets and file folders and typewriter-like keyboards were supposed to make learners comfortable and build on their prior knowledge. In fact, they made desktop computers needlessly complex and difficult for everyone to use except the designers and programmers.

J.M. Carroll was one of a group of psychologists at IBM's Thomas J. Watson Research Center who explored the learning problems presented by the mass introduction of computers. That group wanted to find out how new users went about learning their computers so that they could design better training manuals and help features. They set up a simulated office and brought in experienced secretaries and management professionals who were told to imagine that it was their office with a new computer system. They needed to learn the system well enough to teach their colleagues. The researchers asked the participants to think out loud about what they were trying to do so they could watch and record what happened.

At first the workers were excited and optimistic. They expected quick and easy learning—all they needed to do was follow the instructions that had been provided. But they kept getting sidetracked trying to master other functions, not part of the proposed sequence. That resulted in mess ups that made it impossible to do what they were supposed to be doing. For example, they wanted to number the pages, but ended up with various headers and footers that made it impossible to get back to adjusting the document's margins. In search of answers, they skipped around in the manuals trying to find what they needed to know. When they couldn't locate the relevant information, they made guesses based on their meager prior knowledge, and most of the time that further complicated the problems. Immersed in trying to correct errors, the workers ended up not paying attention to the instructions they were supposed to be following.

As their optimism foundered, anger took over. They criticized the instructions, the manuals, the software, and the machines. Many blamed themselves or cynically dismissed the whole activity. All agreed that the experience made them feel frustrated and stupid. In short, the systematic instructional design failed. The office workers did not like it, rebelled against it, and didn't learn much at all about operating a personal computer.

Carrol saw a pattern in their learning dysfunctions. It was caused by a clash between the systematic step-by-step way the computer designers thought people learned and the active way they actually do. This case illustrates the conflict between learners' desires to take action and their need to do so relying on their current knowledge. The impulse to do makes novel demands on the learner's knowledge. Prior knowledge, however useful its history, produces errors and distortions when applied to new situations. Trying harder to make prior knowledge work in the face of those errors promotes the conflicts and contortions that are the first steps in revision. Novices do need information but systematically spraying them with everything they need to know won't help because it gets filtered and distorted by what they think they know.

"Training wheels," like those that keep kids from falling as they're learning to ride, ended up being the solution Carroll used for those subjects trying to learn computers. He had the engineers devise a word processor interface that blocked access to advanced document functions (like format and merge). This practice system allowed novices to use their knowledge of typing and editing. It enabled them to get started—to do some tasks initially. They made mistakes but not the serious disasters that had previously prevented their progress. Compared with subjects who learned word processing under those structured forms of practice, these subjects started quicker, improved more, reduced the time it took to fix errors, and performed better on comprehension and attitude tests completed afterwards (Carroll, 1990). Mastering the basic functions with fewer error-recovery distractions allowed the learners more time to see how the system worked and develop a better mental model of word processing (Carroll, 1990).

Confronting a new subject is like entering a new world. The new world is a critic dissing assumptions and rejecting guesses. Learners have to find out if they need to change their representations and if so, what they need to change. Learners can't go at the world without any ideas because that would lead to random stumbling and catastrophic failures. Beliefs, however inappropriate, are the working hypotheses that allow learners to make productive errors. A productive error is one that indicates what needs to change. This is the essence of learning by doing.

If instructors design courses to minimize errors, they reduce the likelihood that students will learn. However, students have to expect to make mistakes. If they don't, then frustration and dismay may abort exploration and prevent learning. The faster and more errors students make, the quicker they can learn. When students make, confront, and recover from errors, they learn. That's what deliberate practice is all about—not becoming perfect but eliminating poor strategies and replacing them with ones that work better.

To summarize: Whether students are learning to use a spreadsheet or write poetry, they need to act—as in make a spreadsheet or write a poem. Confronted with a new situation, students will try to apply their expertise to that situation. If what they know doesn't help them create a spreadsheet or write a poem, those failures signal the need to revise their representations. They need information. That failure, or it could be a mistake or error, promotes learning, so we must design learning activities and assignments that make mistakes likely—that put students in a position to learn.

Teaching That Minimizes Information and Maximizes Support for Learning

Roger Schank (2000) notes that, "When people are surprised that they can't solve a problem as they expected . . . they're receptive to helpful information" (p. 223). We're wrong to assume that such failure is permanent and harmful. We should be creating conditions where students can stumble, recognize mistakes, and recover to learn. By facilitating the most useful failures, reducing the harmful costs of failure and eliminating humiliation for failure through design and coaching, we can accelerate the learning process. Carroll urges us to see these initial strategies not as defects that must be remedied, or approach them as embarrassments that must be suppressed, but as fundamental properties of the learning situation.

Offering a design-based approach to learning called *minimalism*, Carroll challenges us to stop obstructing learning with too many instructions, too much reading, and endless explanations. Instead, instructors should minimize information and maximize support for learners' activities. Minimalist principles allow us to demystify errors and incorporate them in our instructional design.

Consider that teachers, trainers, and textbook authors, mostly confront the experiences, strategies, and metaphors students use to investigate new domains by trying to persuade students not to use them. Too often traditional instruction forbids action and vigorously suppresses learners' use of their own knowledge. Hence the prison-like architecture and rules of the classroom. Students must quietly listen, and not do. Or if they do, it must be limited to following the instructor's directions. Lessons in the humanities where I taught typically begin with readings about the history or background of the subject and balloon to pages containing basic terminology, categories, and principles all to be mastered before the learner gets to try anything.

While this sequence reflects our understanding of how learning should be done—understand first, act later, conflicts with how people actually learn. They act first in order to understand if and what needs to change about what is known. In attempting to stifle learner biases, how they think they should go about doing something, traditional instruction signals the brain "no learning here," and students decide the course is irrelevant. In contrast, minimalism views students as people trying to make sense of the learning situation by doing and thinking.

Learning motivates. It produces a sense of euphoria. Our species would not have survived unless we learned continuously. It is impossible for us not to want to learn—despite the frustrations and effort it entails. When we face unmotivated students, we must conclude that our instructional design has suppressed their motivation. If our assignments don't offer students tasks they want to undertake, students won't make the trial and error efforts that learning requires. Carroll (1990) writes, "The most important factor in learning is the learner's motivation, but this is also the factor least amenable to extrinsic control through design. If learners want to undertake a particular activity, letting them try to do it is perhaps the best design step we can take" (p. 8).

The minimalist idea is to get the learner to act in ways that can optimize learning. Instruction, whether delivered orally, in a manual or a text, must capitalize on the students' knowledge and their need to actively improve it. The "doing more with less" minimalist slogan emphasizes doing more learning with less helping. Since errors are a necessary part of the process, instructors can offer learners strategies and support for handling errors. The minimalist instructor wants to promote promising errors and help learners correct them.

Minimalism's first principle, "Provide learners with an immediate opportunity to act" means give students a range of tasks that demonstrates what they can do with new knowledge. The focus is an immediate learning pay off. To provide that quick pay off, minimal instruction must "Begin with a real task that is basic to the subject to be learned." Learning to run a computer is this kind of task. But the designers failed to scale down the problem and give learners a task that resulted in correctable errors—ones that the learners could learn from. The activity or assignment must be doable, understandable, encourage further explorations, but not frustrate and otherwise squelch the desire to learn. The point is not to reduce or block errors but to facilitate and illuminate them so they can be used to explore the limits of what is being learned.

Minimalism suggests that initial learning tasks begin with less conceptual information and more practice. In a critical reasoning course that means working with basic tasks such as creating arguments, mustering evidence, formulating problems, designing solutions, and rejecting or accepting knowledge claims. Never convinced by talk alone, students need experiences to develop mental models. They need permission to act, as well as invitations to explore. Facilitating action is not the same as tossing students into the deep end. Carroll advises that teachers immerse themselves in the world of the student—observe errors, recoveries, and insights.

Problem-based learning, or PBL, illustrates minimalism's second principle, a call for real tasks derived from the content to be learned. In medical schools PBL programs present problems the same way they occur in the world—patients with complaints or symptoms. Thus, the problems worked on in courses are closely related to the kinds of process and ideas that students confront in their clinical training and future practice.

I would grant that it's not as easy to make those kinds of connections in undergraduate subjects, although some of the recent work on wicked problems shows promise (Hanstedt, 2018). Despite the challenges, minimalist teaching is the truest form of learner-centered teaching. It puts students in the driver seat where they will make mistakes, but a teacher rides along with them.

Avoiding Harmful Mistakes

The idea of learning from mistakes seems intuitively obvious and yet impossible. If we think about our first day on a bicycle, the teaching power of mistakes is obvious. But if we think about learning to drive a car, mistakes can be fatal. "There are mistakes," said the jazz great, Thelonious Monk, "and there are notes that don't sound good." The categories of "mistakes" and "failures" are so broad that a mistake can be anything from a missed key stroke to a decision to invade Russia, and a failure can be a lapse of memory, a dropped pass, or a missile exploding on a launch pad. Mistakes, failures, and errors can be destructive, funny, or enlightening. Let's stick with Monk's distinction—there are mistakes that open new possibilities or from which you can learn, and there are mistakes that frustrate and harm.

When we design a learning experience, we want to promote errors from which students can learn and avoid those that can harm them. How can we do this without meddling in the students' exploration? How can we tell which helps and which harms? When Roger Schank (2000) and other cognitive scientists proclaim that we learn from failure they're referring to mistakes that don't harm learners. When teachers are warned to help students avoid mistakes, they are thinking about mistakes that harm. We don't walk in front of cars to learn about safety. We do stammer through Arabic phrases to learn how to speak and understand the language. How should we proceed if we wish to maximize learning—design to avoid harmful mistakes and to encourage mistakes from which learners can recover?

One professor I know avoids directly talking about mistakes and yet he has designed an activity that encourages students to make them. It's a particularly creative approach. He gives students what he calls fake quizzes. He hands out what looks like a normal quiz but presents it as a hypothetical. "Suppose that today's quiz looked like this." Students will proceed to take the quiz under the normal rules; no cheating and books closed. When they finish, he collects their answers and disusses with the students the best and worst solutions, identifying errors in the process. Then he follows this quiz with a second one, similar to the first, but with more complex problems. After completing that quiz, there's more discussion of solutions and mistakes. Finally, there's a quiz that involves material from the previous two but also contains still more complexity. This is the real quiz—the one that counts. "Almost everyone scores high on the last quiz," he has confided, "and they don't make mistakes." He got the idea for the fake quizzes after repeatedly hearing from students that they really understood a problem and its solution after taking a quiz and having a discussion.

Physics professor Eric Mazur (1997) devised another way to exploit mistakes. He used concept tests. After lecturing for several minutes on a concept—for example Archimedes' principle that a body immersed in a fluid is buoyed up by a force equal to the weight of the displaced fluid—he gave the class a quiz: *Imagine holding two identical bricks under water. Brick A is just beneath the surface of the water, while brick B is at greater depth. The force needed to hold brick B in place is larger than, the same as, or smaller than the force required to hold brick A in place.*

The question is designed so that the answer cannot be generated by an equation or recall. Students had only a minute to select an answer and record it. Then he asked students to try to convince someone seated nearby that their answer was correct. Mazur joined in some of these discussions in order to hear the common mistakes students made. After a few minutes of deliberation, students recorded a second, possibly revised, answer. He projected the results of the distribution of answers on a screen and followed that with an explanation of the correct answers and probable reasons for the mistaken answers. The technique offers a way to give students opportunities to think, decide, and fail in a situation in which they have to defend their decision and reasoning but without penalties for failure. Mazur calls this "peer instruction," but it might be more accurate to call it "learning by thinking" or even "fun with failure." It engages students and is effective precisely because it reduces lecture time and increases the students' opportunities to think.

One of the lessons that Caroll (1990) learned in the computer experiments was that teachers should focus less on evaluating learner's first efforts. In fact, if they transferred management and evaluation tasks to students, that promoted further opportunities for discussion and decisions. Ideally, students should make multiple mistakes early in the course and very few close to its end. If we record grades for those early mistakes, we chisel them into the students' evaluation. Effectively we penalize the students' efforts to learn and reward their efforts to avoid it.

There's a hard and harmful way to learn to ride a bike and there is an easier way. I learned the hard way. For my birthday my parents gave me a full-size bike that I could grow into. It was a grey and maroon J.C. Higgins loaded with a headlight, horn, and turn signals. To ride this heavy beauty, I would push off and coast, wrangling the handlebars for balance while my feet searched for the pedals. Then I'd come to a curb, a turn, and tilt wildly. I would try to get my foot on the ground before the bike's bar slammed my crotch. After hours of doing, screwing up, recovering, and getting back on, my beauty of a bike was scratched and banged. The inside of my thighs were black and blue, and my shins were pedal-dented and scratched. I could barely walk. Despite the hard knocks, I did learn to ride a bike.

With training wheels, I could have sailed safely and much less painfully down the street. After several days of practice—provided the training wheels were progressively raised—I could have mastered the body movements necessary to maintain the bike's balance. But training wheels postpone rather than facilitate learning. To balance a bike, you have to shift your weight away from the direction the bike tilts. If the bike doesn't tilt you can't learn, and with training wheels on the bike it doesn't tilt.

There's a better way than my way and training wheels. Start with a small bicycle that allows the rider to put their feet flat on the ground while sitting, take off the pedals, and have the rider use their feel to scooter and coast the bike around an empty parking lot. As soon as the rider can keep the bike balanced, add the pedals. Most children can learn to ride that way in an hour or two.

The beauty of the low-seat-no-peddle arrangement is that the bike can wobble but it won't fall. The rider's errors are learning opportunities. The mistakes aren't suppressed and they don't hurt. Thus it meets Carroll's goal of not eliminating errors and reducing the challenge of learning, but limits the consequences of errors to allow for quick recovery. Training wheels make riding easier but they don't promote learning. Learning to ride a bike happens when the training wheels come off. As teachers we need to design learning experiences that avoid harm and motivate learning.

Imagination: The Response to Failure

Imagination does not find a welcome home in a classroom where transmission and imitation hold sway. Imagination is a doctrinal mystery to many philosophers of science who are careful to distinguish between the testing of ideas, which we can discuss, with the creating of ideas, which we can't. The arts, of course, worship imagination as a product of genius, which you either have or you don't. We delight in the wonderful ideas of physicists, composers, and novelists, but remain awestruck about where those ideas come from and how humans create them.

The novelist, Ursula Le Guinn (2017), wrote that the most frequent question asked of successful writers is "Where do your ideas come from?" Ralph Ellison told her that he told people that he got his ideas from a mail-order company in Schenectady. Assuming that most of us don't have access to that company, where do our ideas—guesses, visions, and patterns—come from? Le Guinn maintains that ideas are how the brain works on the world, imagination wrestling with raw experience to make sense, to tell us a story. We do this to survive—to escape the thralls of past mistakes and the sheer confusion of life.

When we say that the brain represents but doesn't record the world, we mean it creates stories, maps, or models. The stories can be the fiction of a novel, or the model can emerge in a scientific treatise. While both are imagined, that is "made up," they are not arbitrary. They are based on what we already know—that complex amalgam we call "sense." They are selected and stored according to the brain's evolved structures, what the philosopher of science, Norwood Russell Hanson (1958), called "thematic frameworks" or existing preconceptions. Famous for demonstrating that perceptions are theory-laden, Hanson did not see such "stories" as a defect and distortion, but rather as the source of the rich historical connections and patterns on which science is constructed. For him science would not be a powerful way to know if it were not loaded with expectations, goals, theories, and their deep connections.

Ideas come from our experiences reconstituted by our imagination. We make new patterns out of old configurations. According to Le Guinn, it's like composting. It takes heat, time, stirring, water, more vegetable peels, and patience. Play is re-creation. It combines what we know with the novelty we face. The result can be *Moby Dick*, a quantum theory of gravity, or the *Book of Revelation*.

The job of imagination is to tame reality into stories that help us face it and plans that help us control parts of it. The process is long and obscure: Experience must be culled, shaped, fused, reworked, and reborn. The resulting pattern must make sense to others because invention is only the first step in the extensive vetting of ideas that scientists and artists must do before their knowledge can be believed. Both science and literature are communal enterprises involving exposition, criticism, deliberation, correction, rejection, or acceptance.

Imagination is a skill to be developed and nurtured. It requires craft and deliberate practice. To master writing you must write, recognize your failures, and try alternatives to write better. To do science you have to experiment, record your failures, and try new experiments to do better. When seated in a classroom, imagination cannot be watched or heard. Thus, the more we neglect imagination in education the less learning takes place.

In sum, the major work of instructors is to create and evaluate the environments of learning. Teachers are the architects of those figurative and literal spaces in which students learn. This chapter suggests some features of those environments that accelerate the learning; the need for action, for less teaching and more support, and increased respect for imagination. It's a pedagogy based on a culture of criticism and the management of ignorance. It's an approach for which teacher action designs for—and then supports—the actions that students must take in order to discover what they don't know and can learn what they need to know.

References

Carroll, J. M. (1990). *The Nurnberg funnel: Designing minimalist instruction for practical computer skill.* MIT Press.

Dewey, J. (1916). *Democracy and education*. Gutenberg.

Hanson, N. W. (1958). *Patterns of discovery.* Cambridge University Press.

Hanstedt, P. (2018). *Creating wicked students: Designing courses for a complex world.* Stylus.

Le Guin, U. K. (2017). *No time to spare: Thinking about what matters.* Houghton Mifflin Harcourt.

Mazur, E. (1997). *Peer instruction: A user's manual.* Prentice Hall.

Schank, R. (2000). *Coloring outside the lines: Raising smarter kids by breaking all the rules.* Harper Collins.

II

PRACTICE MAKES PERFECT, BUT NOT UNLESS IT'S DELIBERATE

It was a cruel spring day that delights poets. A recent shower made the grass gleam. Balmy air washed the pale sky. And I was 17, as green and full of myself as the swelling buds. After years of indifferent performances in school I was finally recognized as a promising scholar. I went to meet the toughest teacher in the school, David Beckmeyer. He was going to announce that I was the best science student of my graduating class.

Through the windows of the chemistry lab, the afternoon sun burst into rainbows as it hit the glassware. Davey, as we called him, would be cleaning and arranging, or reading at his desk. Brilliant, terse, and demanding, he taught chemistry and physics for 31 years, becoming the best teacher in the school. He was at his desk, in his starched lab coat, and looking at his sacred black grade book. Left standing I waited for him to lift his eyes. They met my face and reduced me to an atom, a molecule, a particle.

"Spence," he said, "you have broken the school and the state examination records in chemistry." I began to smile. "But I don't get you." He opened the grade book. "Look at these." I saw the row of my semester quiz scores: 68, 73, 49, 81, 77 . . . They averaged, I knew, a low "C." "How can you explain that you barely pass the daily quizzes, but on comprehensive and standardized tests you score higher than any student I've ever taught?"

I considered what he wanted me to say. Did he think I cheated? "Well, I think that . . . " I never finished. The prosecutor slammed his hand on the gradebook. "I'll tell you, you are a freak of nature." Davey's voice shot, "You're, you're an idiot savant. You have a photographic memory. You don't respect the scientific method. You don't have discipline. You are not systematic. You think you are smarter than your teachers. But you don't fool me.

I'm not a sucker. You are not outstanding. You will never be a scientist. That's it. That's all."

My face flamed but there was no protest. I fled the dusty bottles and floating motes of the lab. Outside, the lingering winter breeze nipped my arms. I turned the scene over as I walked home. *Was I a freak*? Every teenager faces that fear. I thought not. Yet I liked the photographic memory part. That would make college a breeze. With that thought and the intoxication of a graduating senior with a scholarship to an Ivy League school, I brushed his onslaught away. Still the words stayed with me. Davey was usually right. I couldn't convince myself that he was wrong. What made chemistry so easy? I'll tell you.

It's a tale of practice, failure, and feedback. It all began when I learned to read. The Wright brothers' biography opened a private world of two Ohio engineers puttering away in their bicycle shop introducing me to matter, motion, and best of all, imagination. It beckoned me to venture where failures were always temporary and tomorrow was another chance. I built kites, model airplanes, barometers, and radios. I made oxygen, purple gas, magnetic nails, radios, motors, and hosts of amusing junk. The work of making; the laborious struggles to transform directions into things taught me persistence. My joy in things that flew, flashed, and reeked inspired me to spend hours in basements or garages. From the time I decided I would be an aeronautical engineer, the world of science was my private antischool.

The narrative I told myself was that of a lonely genius making discoveries. Nobody paid much attention or believed his reports, but he eventually triumphed. That was how it was supposed to go. I especially liked the lonely part because it meant freedom. The misunderstood genius part excused my ragged school grades and many failures (the crashed planes, the jars of inert goo, the orange-crate cars that never made it down the hill, or the diagrams I couldn't understand in books where I searched for answers). Best of all the vindicating future promised satisfaction and revenge. So, I tinkered on.

Learning to Problem Solve in the Basement

I started with model planes, from cardboard to wood and paper gliders, rubber-band powered flyers, to full-blown balsa and doped models powered by glow-plug gas engines. It took concentration to align a wing or paint a cowling red. The pattern of work was the same: Build a plane and fly it. If it crashed try to find out why, then repair, correct, or build another plane. Since my funds were limited, the process tested my ingenuity. An avid reader of *Popular Science*, every monthly issue (replete with explanations, diagrams, and helpful workshop hints) kindled my desire to make and understand. I would read the description of, say, a simple electric motor, gather the 25 cents worth of materials, and try to build it. When it didn't work, I would try to find out why and go back to correct the wiring mistakes until I got it to work. Some projects took days and some weeks, depending on resources and skill.

I built crystal radios using the same procedure: Read the description, scrounge the materials, build the device, and try it out. If it didn't, work back up and rebuild. I went on to one-tube radios, simple transmitters, and signal amplifiers to bring in more distant stations. I could broadcast my voice, make siren sounds, bells ring, and red lights spin and flash. All this brought along the knowledge of capacitors, resistors, vacuum tubes, rheostats, generators, motors, and wiring diagrams. Thus, I entered the invisible world where electrons made lights glow, nails become magnets, and radios receive voices from distant places. I was good enough at tinkering, to land a part-time job in a record and appliance store as an apprentice repairman. By my senior year I was taking evening courses in electrical circuits and electronics at the local junior college. Out of sight, in the basement, I lived in a laboratory where I acted as an adult—made decisions and lived with the consequences.

But the most dramatic part of my story lay in a different realm. Billy Corbaugh was the fuse. In a junior high general science class, Billy demonstrated his home-built rocket-bomb. It was so loud and the smoke so thick that it cleared the school before the teachers got everyone under control. Billy was sent home. I went over after school. He took me out to a dilapidated garage where he hid his box marked "Explosives. Keep Out." Inside were several boxes of .22 caliber shots, a can of black powder, matches, and a dozen empty toilet paper tubes. He showed me how to pull the bullets from the .22 casings and empty the powder into the box.

"When I get enough, I pack it into those tubes, fix a fuse, and take it down to the dump to blow something up," he explained.

We became partners, although Billy was more a detonator than a worker. He wanted blasts and soaring tin cans. My job was to figure out how to make combustibles and that was my door into chemistry. I used my standard approach: Find a plan or description, gather materials, mix it up, and fire it up at the dump. The resulting fizzles, duds, or pops sent me back to figure out how to make it work. In the library I found pictures and rough formulas for gunpowder. Billy burned hardwood branches down at the dump and ground them up for charcoal. I bought small bags of saltpeter and sulfur at the drug store. In those days drug stores sold a range of chemicals to kill pests, clean tools, and perk up canned pickles. When the pharmacist queried me about the saltpeter I just said, "Mom needs it." Within weeks we had our first batch of gunpowder. It smoked, but barely fizzled. We mixed the formula more carefully—2 parts potassium nitrate, 1 part sulfur, and 3 parts charcoal. That worked better, blasting bottles and sending toilet paper cylinders high in the air. Billy wasn't satisfied. I headed back to the library where I learned, "the combustible ingredients must be reduced to the smallest possible sizes and as thoroughly mixed as possible." With the aid of Billy's mother's grater, we got it finer and we mixed it more. But still our powder was much weaker than the powder from the .22 shells. Why? In the library I discovered that the manufactured powder was ground quite small, wetted, and then pressed into cakes that were broken into even smaller particles.

It was at that point I started to learn the language of chemistry; K was potassium, S meant sulfur, C carbon, and O was oxygen. Applying a match to gunpowder was: $2\ KNO_3 + S + C \rightarrow K_2S + N_2 + 3CO_2$ or BOOM. The water in the glass was molecules, H_2O. When I produced a rotten egg smell it was H_2S. Hooked I began to build a laboratory in the furnace room of our basement. Billy didn't share my enthusiasm. He didn't like the mixing/grinding drudgery or the duds.

With a collection of jars, bottles, old glassware, discarded tubing, metal scraps, and wires, I tinkered on to fashion stands and clamps of wood scraps. I bent coat hangers and used pretty much any junk I could find. With this junk I built the devices diagrammed in the public library's chemistry books. I would start with a simple device or something I needed like direct current to power my radios. Commercial batteries worked but I couldn't afford them. But friends and family gave me their dead ones. I took them apart and plundered them for carbon, lead, and zinc. The Mason jar battery I devised worked poorly. Impractical, yes, but a prototype that showed me I could create electricity with a chemical reaction.

Over the next 2 years I learned to build batteries, rectifiers, condensers. An old aquarium was converted into a hydrolysis apparatus that made oxygen and hydrogen. I spent an intense hour or two at this almost every day. I had to be patient and careful. A fire, explosion, or blown fuse would put me out of business. Being careful meant close attention to small things like live wires and the difference between H_2SO_4 and H_2SO_3. Mistakes there were, but they had to be corrected. I was wedded to procedures of care and cleanliness and that disciplined me in a way that my parents and teachers would have thought miraculous. Once I had learned to work through these problem-solving routines and recovered from mistakes, I became confident. The principles began to make sense. I just knew that if I kept at my crude laboratory, I'd become a scientist and invent something fantastic. Of course, it didn't work out. My father discovered me making chlorine gas one day and shut down the laboratory.

When I entered Davey's class, I was far from a competent chemist. But I was one hell of a student of chemistry. I had created detailed representations of the electro-chemical world. I did that through countless failed experiments—nonexploding rockets, melted circuits, stinging fingers, and acid holes in my jeans that perplexed my mother. I also learned from eventual success that resulted because I explored mistakes. As a result, I understood and retained detailed information of reactions and molecular structures. I had a complex set of representations that provided a structure for the information I learned. A philosopher might say that I made conjectures—guesses about how to do something—and tested them through trials—not always competent—until I got the results I wanted or met a barrier that made me stop.

I learned basic chemistry through practice. Not the kind that teachers urged on me—repeat, repeat, repeat, until I could recite the textbook. That bored me and killed my curiosity. I faced inexhaustible things that I sought to understand through many tasks and trials repeated again and again. The repetitions were like small aggravating defeats that lead to success. It was almost like cheating; guessing before you knew what you were doing, using the result to guide your response, thinking things through even when it didn't make sense, testing before you were prepared, trying and correcting, in a pattern of adventurous repetition.

Experts would call my approach deliberate practice. It requires retreat into a grueling routine. Much of the work of learning is not intrinsically fun, but as I found out it becomes enjoyable. Each attempt to make something caused trouble that demanded adaptations. Deliberate practice builds habits of intense focus. I learned not in the read-the-principles-and-apply-it way that school prescribed. If you had asked me how I learned, I would have shrugged. I didn't think about what I was doing as learning and that's the power of deliberate practice.

Deliberate Practice

Basement hours making things chemical refined my mental representations. I started with notions like mixing, dissolving, and cooking. Those kitchen models were refined and replaced with ones like acidity, reactions, solvents, and solutions. Then there were compounds, elements, ions, and molecules. New concepts enabled me to see how abstract formulas related to what I was trying to do. Like a net, they caught crucial information swimming in the noise. I started being able to read the periodic table. Pretty soon I could predict results of mixing and heating. The boiling blue liquid in the test tube or the arc of electrons between two carbon sticks generated by a primitive battery were triumphs. Like a lot of kids before me, I discovered chemistry as a way to have frightening fun. I did it for hours without knowing that I was practicing—building knowledge and skills in a deliberate way.

I was not an idiot savant and I didn't have a photographic memory (and that has pretty much been ruled out for humans anyway; Chase & Ericsson, 1982). My hard-won abilities seemed to be a gift or a special fluke as Davey declared. However, it was hours of practice that advanced my memory skills. Studies find that the extended *use* of information leads to better memory (Ericson et al., 1993). The emphasis is on use. If you repeatedly use information in the quest to build or do something, your memory will improve. Use leads to failures—there are always gaps between pristine principles and messy reality. Failures reveal what you don't know and need to know. Searches find information that is relevant—that fits the complex structures of long-term memory. This way I progressed and built my first Leyden jar. I stored electricity in a bottle just as I could store information in my models of the chemical world.

After it was composed, no one could perform Tchaikovsky's 19th-century violin concerto. Now it is a concert workhorse. Before modern times few people could use the differential calculus taught today to freshmen. In highly competitive arenas like dance, chess, and soccer, today's minimal standards were once thought unattainable. The list of outstanding achievements in many areas of endeavor—athletic, artistic, or intellectual—goes on and on. These improvements are too fast for evolution to be at work. Struck by the anomaly, K. Anders Ericsson, a psychology professor at Florida State, along with associates, spent 4 decades exploring extraordinary human performances (Ericsson et al., 1993). He found that astounding abilities resulted more from the quality and quantity of practice than from talent.

Deliberate practice is based on Ericsson's idea that you need to confront your mistakes. If you want to learn, you must work on what you aren't good at. The focus is to improve small weaknesses to achieve great leaps in effectiveness. It consists of arduous, mindful, and sustained attention to errors and experiments with their correction. Done in a problem-solving state of mind, it sets varied and demanding tasks just beyond the learner's immediate capacities. Seeking small gradual improvements in performance, learners recognize errors through immediate feedback and consider better alternatives. This means that whatever your level of natural talent, excellence results through painstaking error-focused practice. Ericsson challenged the notion that talent and genetics determines expert performance—a notion rooted in the ancient dogmas of aristocracy.

Pundits and authors popularized his work in articles and books as the 10-year, 10,000-hour rule of expertise. That glib characterization meant that anyone can become an expert at something if they just practice. A nation of self-helpers and ambitious parents absorbed the rule the way a fire sucks up oxygen. It went viral. Most overlooked the formidable details of his theory of deliberate practice, especially its implications for education.

Deliberate practice focuses on the most difficult and mistake-prone aspects of a process. A major league baseball player hits balls off a tee in order to observe the results of various grips, bat speeds, points of contact, and stances. A chess player reviews past grand master games pitting their own choices of next play against that of masters to explore new solutions. A concert pianist repeatedly plays a sonata thoughtfully, pausing, singing, making notes on the music page, playing error prone passages again and again at different tempos. In all these examples the goal is to improve—not to be perfect or automatic.

Automatic Performance, Not to Be Confused With Deliberate Practice

Practice means several different activities—to do something habitually, to do something professionally, to do things according to a creed, or to try, make mistakes, and find ways to avoid or exploit them. The traditional practice model requires repetition to reinforce connections among sensations, ideas, and actions. It avoids mistakes to reach perfection. Supposedly good habits result. Students memorize multiplication tables before solving problems, develop a vocabulary before writing persuasive essays, or know the facts before they construct arguments. In this view teachers give instructions, create drills, demand downloads, and grade them.

When actors, musicians, and athletes talk about their actions as automatic, they mean they can smoothly deliver the lines, play the notes or put the ball through the hoop. Their performance may feel automatic and look automatic, but it is not. Pounding a bucket of golf balls may relax you but it won't improve your swing. We repeat the decisions and actions of driving so many times that we can easily navigate, enjoy the scenery, talk to passengers, or plan our work day. We don't seem to need to think. But when actions become automatic—mindless, we might say—that gets us into trouble. Isn't inattention what causes most traffic accidents?

The works of great athletes, musicians, scientists, or artists appear effortless—as if performed by beings different than our blundering selves. Since expert performers often don't tell us how they do the wonderful, it is easy to think that they are determined by genetic gifts. Blocking an opponent's blow, returning a serve, or expressing the passion in a Beethoven sonata requires improvisation; to instantly compute the changing values of many variables beset by surrounding noise and make quick decisions. Ericsson's research shows that distinguished performers practice differently to achieve spontaneous mastery. Repetition until automatic takes only about 50 hours and locks in mediocre performances that satisfy most requirements of daily life.

In much of our lives, success depends on the swerve, the quick, and the dramatically different—our ability to adapt and change. Ellen J. Langer (1997) proposes that mindful learning is open to new information and perspectives; mindless learning is entrapped in old categories and responses that ignore novel signals and perspectives. "Being mindless, colloquially speaking is like being on automatic pilot." (Langer, 1997, p. 4) In contrast, Daniel T. Willingham (2009) writes, "There are basic processes (like retrieving math facts or using deductive logic in science) that initially are demanding of working memory but with practice become automatic. Those processes must become automatic in order for students to advance their thinking to the next level" (p. 87). But he also argues that automaticity causes mistakes. Well, yes, if nothing changes; but at work, in the lab, or on a freeway something is always changing.

Deliberate practice satisfies by demonstrating improvement. The costs are high. Working on the wrong tasks wastes time and causes injuries. Plain repetition is easier. The process of actively seeking to make mistakes so that one can evaluate results and try alternatives is taxing. The concentration involved limits sessions to 1 to 1.5 hours at a stretch. Learners must push themselves to their limits for thousands of hours and many years to become outstanding. Concentration on details isn't as fun as play or as rewarding as an outstanding performance. A no-fail practice session makes everyone feel good. "That was a good class" we say, and we mean the students did as well as we expected. But maybe they didn't learn anything. We need to look more closely at deliberate practice to see how we can use it in the classroom.

Deliberate Practice: The Case of Ted Williams

All arms and legs, the skinny kid didn't look like a ball player. But the 20-year-old hit .327, with 31 homers and 145 runs batted in his rookie year. Two years later he became the first player in 11 years to bat over .400 as well as the last player to ever achieve that statistic. Ted Williams set a single season on base percentage mark of .553 that was never beaten in the 20th century. He successfully hit four times out every 10 at bat in a sport in which three out of 10 is the mark of excellence. An average physique and a mediocre fielder, Williams was one of the greatest hitters in the game.

"Teddy Ballgame" obsessively lived baseball. He was what sports writers call a "phenom." They speculated on what special physical traits made him so good. They wrote that he had superman eyes and could see the ball better than others. But his vision wasn't his secret. It was the intense way he practiced. The young Williams played a special game called "Big League" with an amateur coach, Rod Luscomb. It took two players, a bat, a softball with big seams, and a backstop screen with a bar across it. One pitched and one hit facing the backstop. Any hit above the bar was a triple, below scored a double. A grounder past the pitcher was a single. If a player hit the bar and the pitcher didn't catch the rebound that scored a home run. Every three innings the players reversed positions. Williams and Luscomb played versions of the game nearly every day for 7 years. Williams later recalled, "I was so eager to play, and hitting a home run off Rod Luscomb was as big a thrill for me as hitting one in a regulation game. We played for blood" (Bradlee, 2013, p. 43).

Notice the ingenious characteristics of the game. It was competitive, they could see their mistakes, and they kept score. The raised seams on the ball allowed the pitcher to throw curves, drops, screwballs, and knuckleballs. The feedback was immediate. Williams had thousands of times at bat compared to the dozens a player might get in Little League ball. He could experiment with his footwork, bat speed, grip, and swing. He learned the basics under deliberate practice conditions.

In his later years Williams talked and wrote about the art and science of hitting. He believed there was no such thing as a natural hitter. Lack of knowledge leading to uncertainty and fear caused most hitting faults. Experiment, he told young hitters, imitate what better batters do. Hitting required intense observation of the pitchers and their pitches, their habits, strengths, and weaknesses. At bat you had to consider the count, the score, and the game situation. Instead of focusing on hitters' reflexes, strength, quickness, and style, he emphasized thinking—anticipating the pitch type, speed, and location.

Professional sports have changed with much more attention now focused on natural athleticism. Even so, Williams's experiences are reminiscent of the way youngsters learn to talk, the way they easily learn other languages, and their independent methods of reading. The pattern applies to the way diligent writers work to improve their craft, all the methods of the best athletic coaches and the meticulous preparation of professional football quarterbacks. All these types of deliberate practice involve correcting errors on the fly to continuously improve and become self-coaching.

The Role of Coaches in Designing Practices

For the great basketball coach, John Wooden, the purpose of practice was "to provide a foundation on which individual creativity and imagination can flourish" (Wooden & Nater, 2006, p. 61). He asserted that fundamental skills and understanding should be learned concurrently—not repetition first and then high-order thinking later. Practice for Wooden was to apply knowledge. That's because the failures of practice are the player's cues to improvement.

Criticizing routines according to their results helps learners become flexible and creative. Practice under real performance conditions multiplies and exposes mistakes, and mistakes are opportunities to improve. Not just any mistakes will work; they have to be related to crucial aspects of execution. Trivial errors abound in all human efforts; to be obsessed with them borders on pathology. That is one of the places where coaching helps.

A teacher-coach who knows the discipline and the sorts of mistakes that mar execution is invaluable. Coaches can design tasks, specify goals, and provide appropriate settings where frequent errors lead the learner to experiment. Such designs require knowledge of expert performance in the field of study. The teacher must keep in mind what mathematicians, philosophers, or physicists do to succeed. During practice instructors demonstrate errors, suggest corrective alternatives, and push learners to improve. After practice they review results and modify or introduce new activities for the sole purpose of improving specific aspects of an individual's performance by challenging them with new mistakes.

There are various ways to induce mistakes—by painfully slowing down, speeding up, or by doing routines backwards, blindfolded, or with special equipment. In fields like music, theatre, the arts, and athletics these techniques reveal and detoxify mistakes. Teacher-coaches can design smaller models, microworlds, of complex routines that challenge and intrigue learners.

Athletic coaches don't have it all that easy observing a player's execution. It takes great skill to see and understand what blocks success. The best coaches I've encountered design practices to simplify game situations so that players face many problems and errors in short time periods. It isn't enough to just present the problems, players have to own them and understand how solutions contribute to performance in a game. Well-designed practices make the learning visible to both coach and player. For example, small-sided soccer games compress many chances for mistakes and recovery by limiting space, restricting time, and reducing the number of participants. Games like these involve each player in more decisions and actions, increase the energy expended, and demand more attention. Learning is accelerated by the increased amount of mistakes and immediate feedback. Players' performances improve faster. They learn better and they learn more. But it's up to teachers to design those kinds of practice experiences.

Deliberate Practice: Using It to Improve Writing

The habits of teacher questions, lectures, and corrections make learning invisible. To make performances visible they must be broken down into skills. For example, I broke down essay writing into segments: (a) write an opening paragraph that grabs attention and states what the essay will do, (b) create a key argument, and (c) state and support a conclusion with evidence and arguments. The class evaluated introductions by voting on whether that beginning made them "want to read" the essay. They judged arguments on persuasiveness and conclusions on believability. Breaking down writing assignments uncovered routine mistakes like prevalent passive voice, concealed verbs, and incessant prepositional phrases. Unfortunately, the students did not recognize them as mistakes. Students were used to writing and getting credit for long convoluted sentences.

Many scholars argue that you can't teach writing. Grammar, spelling, vocabulary, yes; but not style. They see mediocre writing as the necessary product of democratic education. I struggled with the problem until I discovered *Revising Prose* written by Richard Lanham (1992). He wrote that you can't revise mistakes you don't see. The book was a coaching tool for exposing what he called "lard." Most bad, bureaucratic writing—the style the students imitated—disguises a lack of substance with words; roughly 50% or more useless verbiage. To penetrate the dubious fog Lanham offered a set of rules, called the paramedic method. The method begins with five steps:

1. Circle the prepositions (of, in, about, for, onto, into).
2. Circle the "is" verb forms.
3. Ask *Where's the action? Who is kicking whom?*
4. Put the action into a simple active verb.
5. Start fast—no windups.

For example, a bad night at the fraternity might be described this way in the "official" university announcement of what happened.

It was found that too much was drunk by the brothers on the property throughout the night resulting in some damage to the furniture in the room where games are normally played. (32 words)

If we eliminate the slow windup, "it was found that," and make the verbs active we get:

The drunken brothers trashed the game room. (7 words)

We started by practicing on typical sentences written by administrators and other public officials. Bloated sentences were given to the class to refashion with the goal of slashing the word count by 50% while maintaining or enhancing the meaning. Students enthusiastically applied the technique, but when we applied the method to anonymous student sentences, they revolted. "Don't you see if I cut out those words my sentence is too simple?"

"Exactly," I pointed out, "Now figure out what you really want to say."

After the first struggles students began to enjoy in-class editing. They saw how their writing should look, sound, and what it should mean. Many students made great progress in their style. I wasn't teaching students to write; I was teaching them to practice writing.

It's harder for teachers to imagine how deliberate practice might work when students need to learn skills like critical thinking. Our academic models stress prepractice activities—writing lectures, creating assignments, and providing appropriate academic settings. Practice gets left up to students who, if they do it, mostly do it in isolation and according to their own best ideas. Students need to develop their own capacities to judge and correct their performances which demands an extreme degree of attention and effort, and this is where feedback from their instructors can help. But providing feedback takes time and with all that content to cover chances for practice are limited. The glaring lack of enough opportunities for deliberate practice and the feedback students need to improve indicts the educational system and is yet another way teaching limits learning.

Feedback: It's Origins and Impact

To learn to do something—for example, hit a tennis ball, play a guitar, or catch a bass—individual efforts must be compared against a standard. Learning depends on getting and using the information generated by such comparisons. From that information, learners can discover and correct mistakes. Failures—considered the gap between desired accomplishments and actual results—can create the information used to polish performance. It can also motivate learners to radically change their approach. In my terms, it enables us to throw out inadequate representations and build new ones.

We learn through efforts, mistakes, and the information cycle we call feedback. Some call this trial and error, and lament its seeming randomness and inefficiency. Others are repelled by how much dedication and effort it takes. I submit that it can't be avoided, but it can be done more effectively.

As teachers our goal is to aid the process through well-designed assignments. We should also serve as extra eyes, ears, and minds to offer suggestions that help students narrow the gap between goals and actions.

Walking, a motion so complex that no robot can do it with the easy grace of a 6-year-old, is continuously monitored and adjusted to prevent falling. Talking is not just the projection of sounds but also an ongoing assessment of their effects. And if I can't adjust my blows when they miss or duck my head to keep from getting whacked again, I won't be much of a fighter. If we can't compare what we do with what we intended; we fall, babble, and get thrashed. An engineer would say that we take signals from the results of our actions and feed them back to make adjustments. Indeed, the idea of feedback as a method of control comes from the problem of regulating machines. You can't run a machine like a steam engine without feeding back its output to regulate its inputs. Otherwise, entropy wins—the machine accelerates until it disintegrates.

Early steam engine tenders watched the speed of the engine's flywheel and manually adjusted the amount of steam coming from the boiler. If they attended to other duties or lost concentration, machines blew up. The external loop from machine to tender and back to machine was always erratic. James Watt found that if you added a whirling set of metal balls geared to the flywheel you could, with levers and more gears, connect the balls as they rose and fell under centrifugal force to move a steam valve to open or close. Best of all you could do this continuously with precision. The machine was controlled automatically, resulting in a smooth steady speed. It seemed like magic—a machine in control but without a controller.

The device led people to think in new ways about the issues of controlling and steering various processes. It produced many useful models of how crucial conditions can be regulated in biology, physics, psychology, and sociology. These models are sometimes collected under the general term, *cybernetics*. That was Norbert Wiener's (1948) word for the science of control in animals and machines. A key to all the models was this notion of feedback. He defined it this way: "Feedback is the control of a system by reinserting into the system the results of its performance. If these results are merely used as numerical data for criticism of the system and its regulation, we have the simple feedback of the control engineer. If, however, the information which proceeds backwards from the performance is able to change the general method and pattern of the performance, we have a process which may very well be called *learning*" (author's emphasis).

Cybernetics is the study of how feedback maintains order in the face of chaos. Organized systems from steam engines to backyard squirrels endure only if they can create and use information about their output to control input. Humans and animals have evolved sensors that monitor their biological functions in the same way. To machines we add sensors that select information on performance. In both cases, feedback functions in the broadest sense to produce a temporary and local reversal of the tendency toward disorganization.

The concept of feedback is deceptively simple yet profound. Thinkers struggle to understand its implications for the ways we use information to change and adapt to the vagaries of existence. It is common sense to apply the term to education. Unfortunately, using feedback to describe aspects of teaching and learning has generated much ink and lots of confusion.

The Folly of External Feedback

Educators ignore the theoretical foundations of feedback: Information about the effects of actions compared to a goal must be used to alter the actions in order to close the gap. To ignore the effects of actions and feedback can mean shouting, hugging, bullying, and preaching, along with insults, advice, praise, and grades. Grant Wiggins (2012) notes that "feedback is often used to describe all kinds of comments made after the fact, including advice, praise, and evaluation. But none of these are feedback, strictly speaking" (p. 10). Thus, even though educational research generally supports the notion that teachers should provide more feedback to students, the failure to understand the theory of feedback promotes confusion.

The assumption is that if teachers provide corrective feedback and grade students, they will work harder and learn. There's no firm evidence for this. Despite decades of persuasive criticism, the practice of grading remains an essential aspect of instruction. So ingrained is the habit that even a tenured professor can get in trouble by not grading. Inherent in the practice of grading is the assumption that students don't need to reflect and teachers don't need to evaluate their own efforts. As long as students fill out the worksheets, answer the quiz questions, take the exams, and write papers, teachers will grade their work. The grades report what has been done, not what could be done. They may identify gaps between students' performances and academic standards but that's the extent of what they contribute.

Wiggins points out that grading is useless as actionable feedback. There's nothing a student can do about a grade, other than register complaints. Still we grade on. Most studies show that the quality of instructor comments does not motivate students to act on what teachers recommend. By the time they reach the university, students have had years to learn the grading system and how to manipulate it. Grades they know; understanding how to use feedback is an enigma.

Most of the feedback literature deals with improving the grading skills of teachers—how to provide more grading opportunities, grade efficiently with rubrics, make useful comments, make fewer or more comments, and sugar-coat threats with encouraging words. The purpose of the feedback is often no more than justification for the grade given. They explain the reasons for this grade, not what the student needs to do to earn a better one. As a result, information conveyed by grades and comments aren't used by many students or even instructors in a systematic way. That a lot of students don't pick up graded exams and papers can be taken as evidence that the grades and comments don't convey useful information. When students do show up at office hours to discuss their graded assignments, most often they're there to see if they can get the grade changed, not to explore how they can improve.

My expectation was that students would struggle on early assignments but gradually improve until their performance met my standards in the last weeks. I wanted them to use grades as feedback to improve. That approach caused anguish. I tried to drop grading until the end of the course, but that raised anxiety levels still higher.

If student brains were plastic and could be molded, all this grading would make sense. But remember, brains don't work that way. They *select* the information they need to use, maintain, or revise their representations of reality. As selectional systems, they depend on feedback to survive and what a grade provides is inadequate. Information about the difference between the purpose of an action and its results is fed back to adjust the action or to take a novel approach to close the gap. Feedback requires a loop from purpose, action, and results, to adjustments or innovation and back again. That's how brains learn.

Feedback is information about the gap between what happened and what's supposed to happen. Reducing the gap requires the selection of new information to apply, maintain, or revise cognitive representations of reality. At a minimum, the representation can be affirmed giving students more confidence in their use of it to guide action. Conjectures and searches are in order until a revised representation emerges. Then the process starts again.

A teacher-coach who knows the discipline and the sorts of mistakes that mar execution is invaluable. Coaches can design tasks, specify goals, and provide appropriate settings where frequent errors lead the learner to experiment. This is important since it implies that feedback is most effective when the student generates the data, does the comparison, and acts to narrow the gap. Wiggins writes that feedback "must be goal-referenced, tangible and transparent; actionable, user-friendly (specific and personalized); timely, ongoing and consistent." Let me break that down and share the details of what a teacher-managed feedback loop requires.

- Goal-referenced information tells the learner if they are narrowing the gap between results and target. "Try harder," won't do. "Reduce the verbal lard by 50%," will.
- Students must be able to see, hear, or feel the information.
- Students relate the information to their intended goals.
- Actionable information means students can understand and use it to make choices. Not "your writing bores readers" but "your sentences average 18 words in length."
- Too much or too technical information won't work. User-friendly feedback can be understood and used at once. "Try eliminating the passive voice" instead of "Your sentences are awkward."
- Timely feedback comes before the end of the performance to provide opportunities to rework assignments again and again.
- Consistent feedback requires accurate trustworthy information.
- Students need multiple chances to learn from their errors. Instructors need a repertoire of assignments and follow-ups to promote and support the chance to learn from mistakes.

Most teachers who examine what's needed to create and maintain external feedback loops will shudder at the demands. There is not enough time in the standard course schedule for such schemes. "No time to give and use feedback actually means, no time to cause learning," Wiggins (2012) cautions. That doesn't mean that students absolutely won't learn. But the learning process will produce predictable random bell curve results. The external feedback model underpinning grading is impractical; "The amount and type of feedback that can realistically be given is severely limited by resource constraints and . . . the expectation of not 'spoon-feeding' students" (Boud & Molloy, 2013, p. 703).

Just as the workers who tended the early steam engines provided an external loop, theoretically teachers can do the same. But the energy and efforts required doom the enterprise. It also robs students of the opportunity to learn how to develop and manage their own feedback. Frequent extensive teacher feedback derails deliberate practice. Too much specific detailed feedback promotes compliance and avoidance in students. It assumes that students can improve by following directions. Where we do see such external loops in action at the highest levels of athletic competition, each learner requires dozens of experts to achieve improvement. It is a testimony to human grit that many instructors attempt to do this. But it is a folly since external feedback systems have the unintended consequence of rendering students eternally dependent, unable to master their own learning.

Self-Coaching: The Internal Feedback Loop

The alternative is self-monitoring or self-coaching; an internal feedback loop. In this model, students set goals, measure results, establish there's a gap between results and goals and try different ways to close the gap. That is one way to conceive of active learning. Given our traditional teaching habits, that model seems wishful at best. But it is economical. "Less teaching more feedback. Less feedback that comes from you and more tangible feedback designed into the performance itself" (Wiggins, 2012, p. 13).

Feedback should be judged by its impact on learning, not in terms of inputs like frequency, tone, and volume. Boud and Molloy (2013) make the point that teachers and students must both be involved. Feedback is a two-way process. Since it isn't feedback if students don't use the information to improve, students have to be involved. Setting goals that students don't care about undermines the process. Instructors can conjecture about what students need to know about their performance, but it takes dialogue and debate to find out what they actually need and can use. Ultimately to be called feedback, it must be based on evidence that students understand and use to improve.

Students must act on information to complete the loop. That doesn't mean faculty can only watch and hope. They can negotiate goals, help develop metrics to measure the gap, and suggest alternative ways to close it. Feedback must become a basic component of course design. Since grading drains the teacher's time to design assignments, monitor results, and make improvements, its importance must be downgraded. Ultimately instructors can best aid the feedback process by designing assignments with clear relevant objectives, and redesign them in light of students' learning. That requires sophisticated disciplinary knowledge and knowledge about the biological and psychological processes of learning. All that's demanding, but the acquisition and correction of such knowledge is the exciting intellectual core of teaching.

Using feedback to perform is a characteristic of every normal human brain. I couldn't walk or pick up my coffee mug without it. Further, I couldn't communicate without watching, sensing, and hearing the responses of my audience. Luckily I usually accomplish those tasks. I can get from the bed to the kitchen, the mug gets to my mouth, and my attempts to communicate humor set off laughter. It seems almost effortless. Self-coaching works. If students made and used internal feedback loops it would transform classrooms.

That transformation begins when students own the feedback. It has to be their perception of a need to change and their willingness to do so that drives improvement. The self-coaching student wants to face mistakes and correct them. He or she demands accurate measures of their performances. They seek and respond to criticism rather than praise. We all have a good sense that the advice "increase your efforts and try harder" is useless. Learners need to know how big the gap is between performance and goal, but they need to know more. What's causing the gap; ignorance, bad habits, or lack of skill? And how might they fill the gap—what they can do to improve. Feedback is motivating. That is one of the reasons humans seek it.

We all know that learning requires practice and feedback. But our thinking about both is vague. Practice as repetition doesn't capture the subtleties of deliberate practice or challenge instructors to design the assignments and situations that motivate students to practice. Games, exercises, microworlds, or simulations take intelligent collective effort; the creation, selection, and application that lurks in the phrase "trial and error." Both students and instructors require internal feedback loops to improve and to experience the joy it brings.

And that brings me to my final question. Can we reimagine teaching as an intellectual venture much like that of successful coaching? The major barriers are culturally endorsed teaching habits—lectures, grades, too many comments, too much advice, and the suppression of errors and student questions. Those habits flow from the deepest conviction that education is about transmitting knowledge. The drum beat of more content delivery drowns the concerns of providing students with opportunities to develop internal feedback and become adept at deliberate practice.

References

Boud, D., & Molloy, E. (2013). *Feedback in higher & professional education: Understanding and doing it well.* Routledge.

Bradlee Jr., B. (2013). *The kid: The immortal life of Ted Williams.* Little Brown and Company.

Chase, W. G., & Ericsson, K. A. (1982). Skill and working memory. In G. H. Bower (Ed.), *The psychology of learning and motivation* (Vol. 16; pp. 1–58). Academic Press. https://doi.org/10.1016/S0079-7421(08)60546-0

Ericsson, K. W., Krampe, R. T., & Tesch-Romer C. (1993). The role of deliberate practice in the acquisition of expert performance. *Psychological Review, 100*(3), 363–406. https://graphics8.nytimes.com/images/blogs/freakonomics/pdf/DeliberatePractice(PsychologicalReview).pdf

Langer, E. J. (1997). *The power of mindful learning.* Addison Wesley.

Lanham, R. (1992). *Revising prose.* Macmillan.

Wiener, N. (1948). *Cybernetics, or control and communication in the animal and the machine.* Technology Press.

Wiggins, G. (2012). Seven keys to effective feedback. *Educational Leadership, 70*(1), 10–16. https://pdo.ascd.org/lmscourses/PD13OC005/media/FormativeAssessmentandCCSwithELALiteracyMod_3-Reading2.pdf

Willingham, D. T. (2017). *Why don't students like school?* Jossey-Bass.

Wooden, J., & Nater, S. (2006). *John Wooden's UCLA offense.* Human Kinetics.

EPILOGUE

Maryellen Weimer

In his 2001 widely cited article, "The Case Against Teaching," Larry recounts a conversation with a student who's taking a course in which student teams explore realistic problems. The student has high praise for the course, "I have never learned so much in a class." Larry comments that the professor must be a wonderful teacher. The student laughs, "Oh, he doesn't know how to teach. He just assigns the problems—we do all the work." Larry writes, "If professors don't talk and test, the result is the same incredulous response from students" (Spence, 2001, p. 11).

Educators continue to resist change because we "share an unshakable image of what teachers and students are supposed to do" (Spence, 2001, p. 12). Larry grabs that image by the neck and shakes it hard. A host of efforts to improve teaching have, "washed through the educational system leaving puddles of improvement" but no change in the fundamentals (p. 12). Most teachers still transmit knowledge which students, with varying degrees of success, memorize and pass back.

Larry wants teachers to coach—to be there on the sidelines while students play the learning game. His coaching teachers creatively design practice sessions that contain educational experiences structured to improve how students learn. They're sessions that raise questions, trip students up, and let them fail, because when students are confronted with what they can't do or don't know, that motivates them to fix, find out, and do better. Action is an ever-present part of the equation. Students learn by doing—it's the crucible that tests the validity of what they know.

Coaching teachers may be on the side lines, but they're very much in the game and heavily invested in the outcome. They want students playing the learning game to win and by ever widening margins. These coaches never take their eyes off students, in the game or during practice. They point out what isn't working or needs improvement. They offer suggestions. They provide support. They don't give answers but encourage students to ask questions.

Many of the teaching problems Larry identifies result from the failure to understand learning. Cognitive science continues to sort out brain functions—specifically, how the brain learns, which it does without teachers and most dramatically in the very young. Recall Larry's joyful account of how his son Duncan learned knobs. The brain does not preserve reality like a tape recorder or a camera. Instead, it selects from the myriad of stimuli details that it configures as representations—maps, models, or narratives, as Larry describes them, that then become understandings of what's happening or explanations of how something works. When something does happen that isn't understood or can't be explained, learners seek more information and use it to change their representations. Larry's not proposing that we do away with teachers—he just wants us to teach in ways that fit with how brains learn.

Larry was a learner like few I've ever known. He had 78 books checked out from the Penn State Library when he died. His interests went in all directions. Driven by curiosity, he looked for answers and the ones he liked best he found in places where none of the rest of us would think to look. That's one of the reasons this book is so interesting to read. But all his interests were superseded by his quest to figure out how learning works and what teaching should be contributing to the process.

What he comes to understand about education, Larry believes with strong convictions. He's figured out what's wrong, and he's got his arms and heart wrapped around a better way. That becomes the great paradox of the book. It rests on the premise that learners must build knowledge for themselves—learn to read, as Larry did, his way. The case Larry constructs for a radically different kind of teaching obligates him to give teachers freedom to build their own representations, to arrive at and act on their own understandings. He passes his book to you—it's in your hands. Put it on the shelf or act on it.

Reference

Spence, L. D. (2001, November/December). The case against teaching. *Change, 33*(6), 11–19. https://doi.org/10.1080/00091380109601822

INDEX

What Inclusive Instructors Do

Principles and Practices for Excellence in College Teaching

Tracie Marcella Addy, Derek Dube, Khadijah A. Mitchell, and Mallory E. SoRelle

Foreword by Buffie Longmire-Avital and Peter Felten

This book uniquely offers the distilled wisdom of scores of instructors across ranks, disciplines, and institution types, whose contributions are organized into a thematic framework that progressively introduces the reader to the key dispositions, principles, and practices for creating the inclusive classroom environments (in person and online) that will help their students succeed.

The authors asked the hundreds of instructors whom they surveyed as part of a national study to define what inclusive teaching meant to them and what inclusive teaching approaches they implemented in their courses.

The instructors' voices ring loudly as the authors draw on their responses, building on their experiences and expertise to frame the conversation about what inclusive teachers do. The authors in addition describe their own insights and practices, integrating and discussing current literature relevant to inclusive teaching to ensure a research-supported approach.

Inclusive teaching is no longer an option but a vital teaching competency as our classrooms fill with racially diverse, first-generation, and low-income and working-class students who need a sense of belonging and recognition to thrive and contribute to the construction of knowledge.

The book unfolds as an informal journey that allows the reader to see into other teachers' practices. With questions for reflection embedded throughout the book, the authors provide the reader with an inviting and thoughtful guide to develop their own inclusive teaching practices.

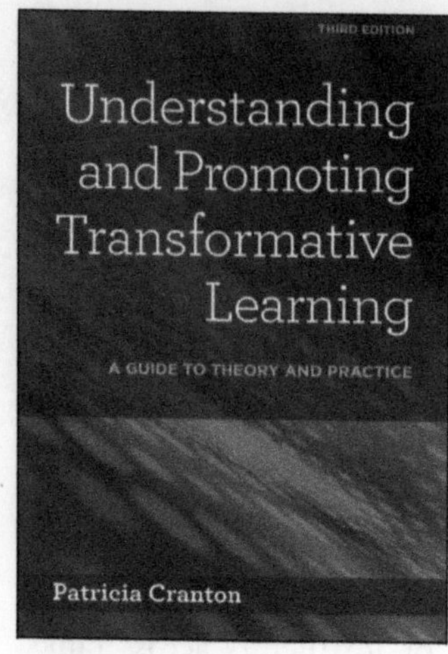

Understanding and Promoting Transformative Learning

A Guide to Theory and Practice

Patricia Cranton

Third Edition

The third edition of Patricia Cranton's *Understanding and Promoting Transformative Learning* brings a wealth of new insight from the tremendous growth in the field during the decade since the previous edition. As in the previous editions, the book helps adult educators understand what transformative learning is, distinguish it from other forms of learning, and foster it in their practice. The first part of the book is dedicated to clarifying transformative learning theory and relating it to other theoretical frameworks. The author examines transformative learning from the learner's perspective, and discusses individual differences in how learners go through the process. In the second half of the book, the focus is squarely on strategies for promoting transformative learning in a wide variety of adult and higher education contexts. Practitioners will be able to take ideas from the text and apply them directly in their teaching.

Since 1975, transformative learning has become a core theoretical perspective in adult and higher education, and research has proliferated. In the past decade, adult education and especially transformative learning grew into a noticeably larger field. The numbers of undergraduate and graduate programs in adult education have increased and continue to increase as more and more individuals are seeking the expertise, skills, and training necessary to work with adult learners in higher education, business, industry, government, health professions, nonprofit organizations, and community development. In addition, the number of programs in higher education (both undergraduate and graduate) that include courses in transformative learning has grown dramatically. These academic audiences use the book to further their understanding of transformative learning theory and practice.

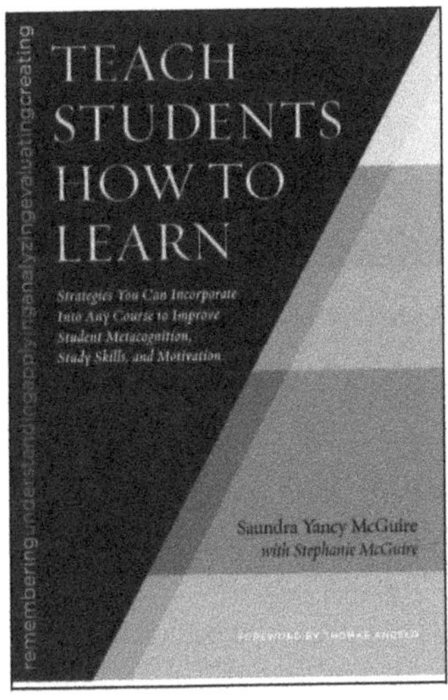

Teach Students How to Learn

Strategies You Can Incorporate Into Any Course to Improve Student Metacognition, Study Skills, and Motivation

Saundra Yancy McGuire

With Stephanie McGuire

Foreword by Thomas Angelo

Copublished with NISOD and NADE

"This book is a wonderful resource for college faculty. It provides us with practical, yet powerful learning strategies and metacognition techniques that can be easily incorporated into our courses, and which in turn, will improve student learning. The author shares both research and her personal experiences, as well as her expertise in teaching all kinds of diverse students with tremendous success. This book is a welcome addition for the postsecondary teaching and learning field and should be read and utilized by all." —***Kathleen F. Gabriel**, Associate Professor, School of Education, California State University, Chico*

"Based on solid scientific theory and real classroom case studies, McGuire's workshop on metacognition provides the participants with sound pedagogical advice and an impressive array of ready-to-use, result-oriented teaching techniques for a 21st-century classroom. With a metacognitive approach to teaching and learning, everything comes together."—***Irina Ivliyeva**, Associate Professor of Russian, Missouri University of Science and Technology*

"An electrifying book! McGuire demonstrates how learning strategies can improve learning—and then charges faculty to teach them, complete with the slides for doing so in your class . . . A must-read—and must-do—for every teacher who struggles with students who don't learn as much as they could or should!"—***Tara Gray**, Director, The Teaching Academy*

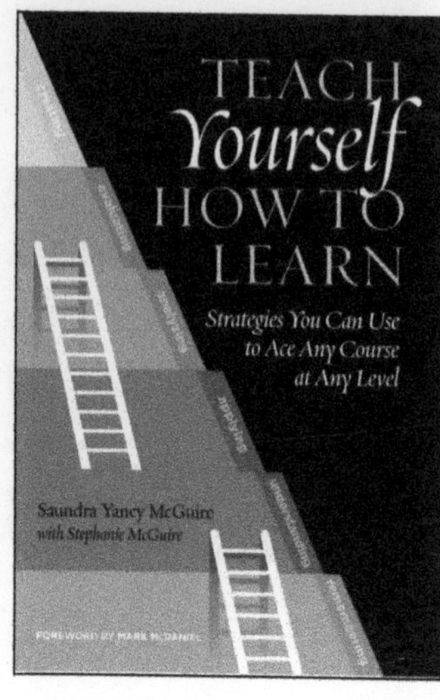

Teach Yourself How to Learn

Strategies You Can Use to Ace Any Course at Any Level

Saundra Yancey McGuire With Stephanie McGuire

Foreword by Mark McDaniel

Following up on her acclaimed *Teach Students How to Learn*, that describes teaching strategies to facilitate dramatic improvements in student learning and success, Saundra McGuire here presents these "secrets" direct to students.

Her message is that "Any student can use simple, straightforward strategies to start making A's in their courses and enjoy a lifetime of deep, effective learning."

Beginning with explaining how expectations about learning, and the study efforts required, differ between college and secondary school, the author introduces her readers, through the concept of metacognition, to the importance and powerful consequences of understanding themselves as learners. This framework and the recommended strategies that support it are useful for anyone moving on to a more advanced stage of education, so this book also has an intended audience of students preparing to go to high school, graduate school, or professional school.

In a conversational tone, and liberally illustrated by anecdotes of past students, the author combines introducing readers to concepts like Bloom's taxonomy (to illuminate the difference between studying and learning), fixed and growth mindsets, as well as to what brain science has to tell us about rest, nutrition, and exercise, together with such highly specific learning strategies as how to read a textbook, manage their time, and take tests.

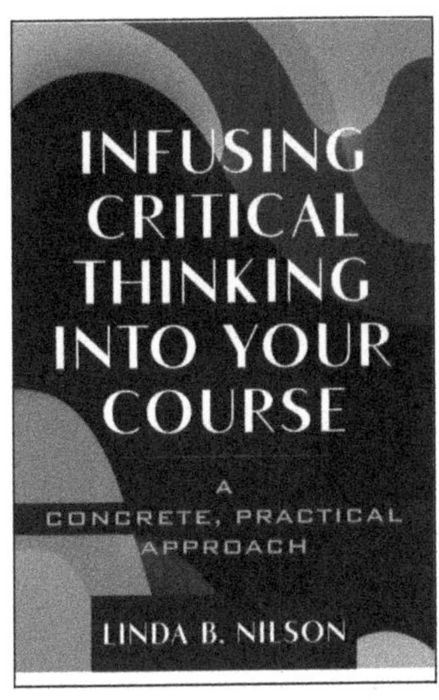

Infusing Critical Thinking Into Your Course

A Concrete, Practical Approach

Linda B. Nilson

"This book should be read and used by every faculty member. Improved critical thinking is an essential outcome for all courses and for research training in any field. Nilson has drawn on her long experience as an outstanding faculty developer to make it easier for any of us to foster advanced critical thinking. She clearly explains the underlying rationale and provides powerful ways to engage students. She includes: (a) a quick and accurate review of major alternative frameworks, (b) extensively developed examples of ways to implement each of them with students, and (c) multiple approaches to assess students' thinking while fostering further sophistication. I would have been a much more effective teacher if I had had this foundation to build on."—***Craig E. Nelson***, *Professor Emeritus, Biology, Indiana University*

"The ability to think critically is vital to our capacity to 'routinely confront dishonesty' in Linda Nilson's words. In this lively and accessible book, Nilson reviews how students can be helped to investigate claims made across a wide range of disciplines. She provides numerous examples of classroom exercises and assessment formats for college teachers seeking practical guidance on how to infuse critical thinking across the curriculum."—***Stephen D. Brookfield***, *Distinguished Scholar, Antioch University*

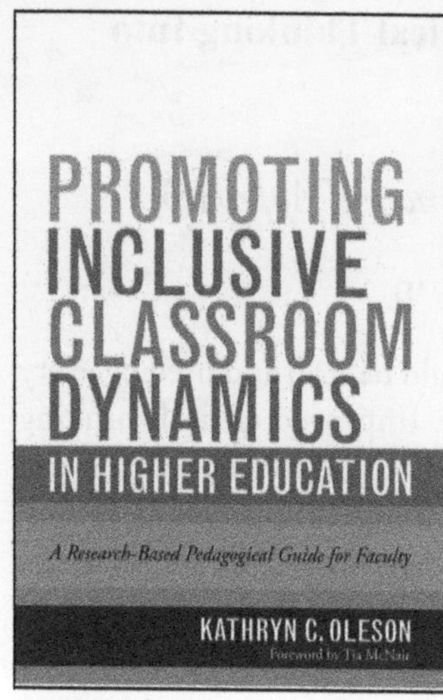

Promoting Inclusive Classroom Dynamics in Higher Education

A Research-Based Pedagogical Guide for Faculty

Kathryn C. Oleson

Foreword by Tia McNair

"Presenting research, strategies, and lived experiences in engaging and accessible ways, Kathryn C. Oleson invites us to reflect on ourselves as facilitators of learning, to recognize the necessity and not just the benefits of more equitable and inclusive classrooms, and to dedicate ourselves to transforming our thinking and our practices. She provides an impressively wide range of conceptual frameworks, concrete approaches, and helpful examples that can guide the necessarily ongoing work of promoting inclusive classroom dynamics."—***Alison Cook-Sather***, *Professor of Education; Director Peace, Conflict, and Social Justice Concentration; Director Teaching and Learning Institute*

This powerful, practical resource helps faculty create an inclusive dynamic in their classrooms, so that all students are set up to succeed. Grounded in research and theory (including educational psychology, scholarship of teaching and learning, intergroup dialogue, and social justice theory), this book provides practical solutions to help faculty create an inclusive learning environment in which all students can thrive.

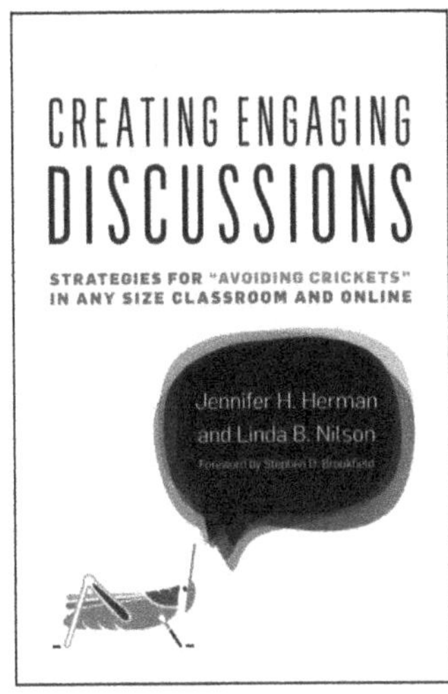

Creating Engaging Discussions

Strategies for "Avoiding Crickets" in Any Size Classroom and Online

Jennifer H. Herman and Linda B. Nilson

Foreword by Stephen D. Brookfield

"*Creating Engaging Discussions* examines one of the most challenging parts of teaching—designing and managing discussion activities that engage students while contributing meaningfully to their learning. Faculty members will love the way the book addresses their common instructional challenges with a mix of evidence-based principles, use-it-on-Monday activities, and in-depth case studies. Educational developers will appreciate its scholarly background and suggestions for using the book within reading groups and workshops. A must-have addition for your bookshelf."—***Greg Siering**, Director, Center for Innovative Teaching and Learning, Indiana University Bloomington*

If you have ever been apprehensive about initiating classroom discussion, fearing silences, the domination of a couple of speakers, superficial contributions, or off-topic remarks, this book provides strategies for creating a positive learning experience.

Jennifer H. Herman and Linda B. Nilson demonstrate how to create the conditions to facilitate deep and meaningful learning as well as to assess the effectiveness of discussions. They identify, analyze, and solve common problems in both classroom and online discussions and in both small and large classes. They take a direct, practice-oriented approach that—in acknowledging common challenges—provides principles, guidance on design, examples of activities and techniques, and eight detailed case studies. These cases demonstrate successful approaches that faculty across disciplines and from a variety of institutions have adopted in their face-to-face, blended, or online courses at the undergraduate or graduate level.

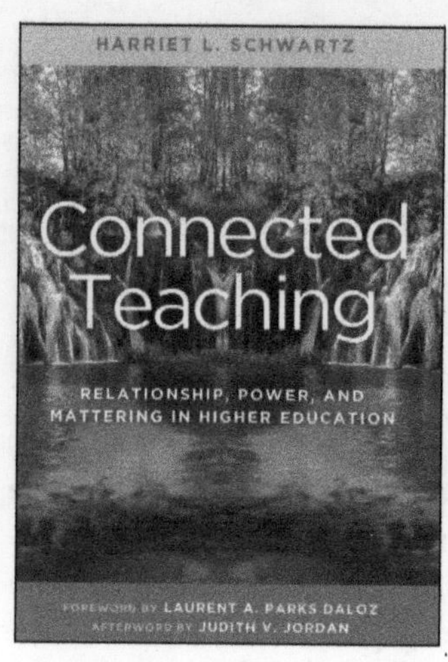

Connected Teaching

Relationship, Power, and Mattering in Higher Education

Harriet L. Schwartz

Foreword by Laurent A. Parks Daloz

Afterword by Judith V. Jordan

"Harriet Schwartz has provided a welcome and much needed contribution in our current educational climate of alienation and fragmentation. As we come to understand how connections and disconnections shape the teaching and learning enterprise, we learn to be increasingly in touch with and value the risks and rewards, the delights and dilemmas that fuel our passion for the academic life."—***Gregg Wentzell,*** *Assistant Director, Center for Teaching Excellence, Miami University and Associate Director, Lilly Conference*

"Harriet Schwartz has provided an open door for all who are interested in rediscovering the importance of teaching as a relational practice. Teaching (in higher education and elsewhere) has always been a difficult task, but changes in technology, student expectations, and other aspects has created an even more challenging undertaking. However, the core aspect of teaching has always been in building relationships between the teacher and the student—no matter what additional technological tools are available. Schwartz presents us with new ways to think about connected teaching and the value of understanding relational cultural theory in the context of 21st-century education."—***Catherine M. Wehlburg,*** *Dean; Sciences, Mathematics, and Education; Marymount University*

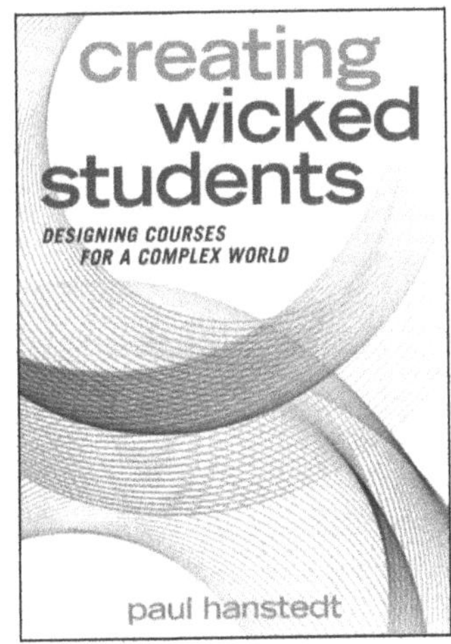

Creating Wicked Students

Designing Courses for a Complex World

Paul Hanstedt

"From its playful title to its final chapter, *Creating Wicked Students* offers a thought-provoking new approach to course design focused on helping college students develop the abilities and self-authorship needed to work—and live—meaningfully. Hanstedt guides the reader through a design process for courses where students learn skills and content, but more significantly, develop 'the ability to step into a complex, messy world and interact with that world in thoughtful and productive ways.'"—***Deandra Little**, Director, Center for the Advancement of Teaching and Learning, and Associate Professor of English, Elon University*

"*Creating Wicked Students* is one of the best books I have read in the past decade. I am a midcareer teacher educator and scholar in an English department, and I wish I had read this book when I was a doctoral student. Nevertheless, this outstanding text has a lot to offer for all scholars trying to adapt to changing technologies and learner populations, providing innovative and practical strategies for course design.

The main argument of the book centers around the idea that we live in a changing, unpredictable world where the demands and expectations placed on graduates are constantly changing. According to Hanstedt, 'we need wicked graduates with wicked competencies,' which he argues are developed when students are provided with opportunities to apply and use information instead of just receiving it. In a highly accessible and reader-friendly way, Hanstedt explains how this is done. He innovatively illustrates how to build such measurable, clear, and meaningful goals for learning outcomes.

In conclusion, this is a must-read for anyone teaching at the college level. The book provides incredibly useful information not only for current faculty but also for doctoral students who will soon assume faculty positions. Paul Hanstedt provides a compelling and thoughtful argument throughout the book that we, college instructors, need to reconsider the skills, goals, concepts, teaching methods, and assessment techniques in our classrooms so that our students, no matter what field they are in, are equipped with the skills, strategies, and knowledge necessary to face the daunting challenges of life after college."—***Teachers College Record***

Also available from Stylus

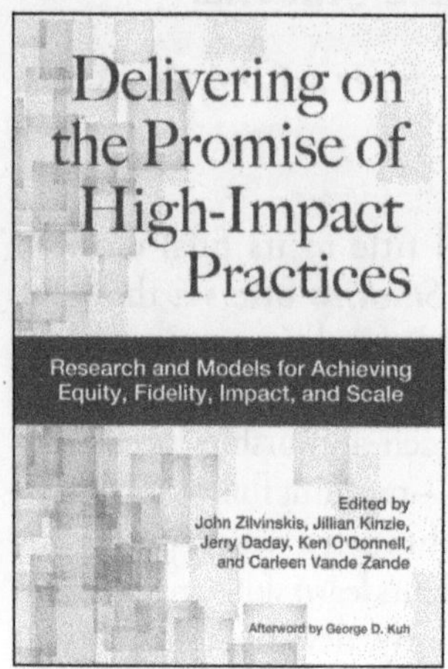

Delivering on the Promise of High-Impact Practices

Research and Models for Achieving Equity, Fidelity, Impact, and Scale

Edited by John Zilvinskis, Jillian Kinzie, Jerry Daday, Ken O'Connell, and Carleen Vande Zande

Research shows that enriching learning experiences such as learning communities, service-learning, undergraduate research, internships, and senior culminating experiences—collectively known as high-impact practices (HIPs)—are positively associated with student engagement; deep, and integrated learning; and personal and educational gains for all students—particularly for historically underserved students, including first-generation students and racially minoritized populations.

While the potential benefits of HIPs for student learning, retention, and graduation are recognized and are being increasingly integrated across higher education programs, much of that potential remains unrealized; and their implementation frequently uneven.

The goal of *Delivering on the Promise of High-Impact Practices* is to provide examples from around the country of the ways educators are advancing equity, promoting fidelity, achieving scale, and strengthening assessment of their own local high-impact practices. Its chapters bring together the best current scholarship, methodologies, and evidence-based practices within the HIPs field, illustrating new approaches to faculty professional development, culture and coalition building, research and assessment, and continuous improvement that help institutions understand and extend practices with a demonstrated high impact.

For proponents and practitioners this book offers perspectives, data, and critiques to interrogate and improve practice. For administrators it provides an understanding of what's needed to deliver the necessary support.

22883 Quicksilver Drive
Sterling, VA 20166-2019

Subscribe to our email alerts: www.Styluspub.com